C000009712

More Stories that Heal

More Stories that Heal

Michael Buckley

daybreak
London

First published in 1992 by
Daybreak
Darton, Longman and Todd Ltd
89 Lillie Road, London SW6 1UD

© 1992 Michael Buckley

ISBN 0–232–51994–3

A catalogue record for this book is available
from the British Library

Most of the Scripture quotations are taken from the
Jerusalem Bible, published and copyright 1966, 1967 and 1968,
or the New Jerusalem Bible, published and copyright 1985, by
Darton, Longman and Todd Ltd, and Doubleday & Co Inc
and used by permission of the publishers

Cover: photograph by Graham Topping;
design by Elizabeth Ayer

Phototypeset by Intype, London
Printed and bound in Great Britain at
the University Press, Cambridge

To 'El Shaddai'
The God of the Mountains
who speaks to us

Contents

Contents

Introduction

'El Shaddai' is the name of our Christian Movement for Inner Healing. 'El Shaddai' is Hebrew and means the God of the Mountains.

The name has always fascinated and inspired me, not only because of the significance of the setting of the mountains in which God sees himself, but mainly because it brings to my mind the story of Abraham. It is a story from the life of someone who lived six thousand years ago which still has the power to thrill and challenge us. When he was ninety-nine years old God appeared to Abraham and said, 'I am El Shaddai' (Genesis 17:1). Even though he was old, Abraham accepted without question God's invitation to start a new life in a strange land. The rest is history. Abraham became known in the process as the father of all those who walk in faith.

The Bible is full of stories of people like Abraham who walked in faith. Jesus is the perfect example of the faithful Son of God. His life is filled with stories of people whom he met and healed through God's power. Healing took him, as it takes all who minister in his name, into strange territory where their lives are transformed, as are those whom they meet. El Shaddai still calls his people to a new life.

In this little book I recount stories that I hope will heal, often stories of people whom I met in my journey through life whose encounter changed us both. I first told these stories on Pause for Thought on BBC's Radio 2. They are recorded here so that you too might draw inspiration from the people about whom I write. They are ordinary people whom God has touched in a simple and beautiful way. What they did inspired the prayers at the end of each story. El Shaddai speaks to many people in our busy world today and they answer his call. Perhaps as you read these stories he may speak to you, and you will do the same.

Friendship

As the Father has loved me so I have loved you. You are my friends. I shall not call you servants any more, because a servant does not know his master's business. What I command you is to love one another. (John 15: 9, 14, 15, 17)

One of the most precious gifts in life is friendship. Without it the world around us becomes a desert of loneliness. Some people find themselves without friends and so wander through life unloved and unloving. It is almost impossible to make any meaningful contact with them because they fail to understand what true friendship really means. Perhaps they have been emotionally hurt in their youth to such an extent that they distrust everyone and so remain on the outside of life, always looking in but never actually taking part. They are not selfish so much as lacking the courage to take a step towards another in friendship. This is basically because they are afraid of being rejected, and who can blame them? They have been rejected many times before, so why should they believe that they are not going to be rejected again when, in their eyes, 'so-called' friendship is once more being offered to them? I

1

think the main reason they fail to respond to friendship is because they have never had love shown to them, never been appreciated for what they are in themselves.

It is not good for man to be alone, God said, because a person who is alone is not fully living. Deep inside each one of us, young and old, there is a power created for love and friendship. We need someone other than ourselves to set that power in motion. It is just like turning the key in a car to start the engine. The engine is there all the time but it needs to be switched on. We have to trust someone to switch on, to awaken, the power within us, but we are afraid to take the risk, afraid to trust ourselves to them. So we lock the door within us that leads to the power, to love, and so friendship never comes to life for us. We condemn ourselves to live in perpetual darkness, living for ourselves and therefore not really living at all.

The world is full of lonely people. The greatest gift we can offer to another is the gift of friendship. When we reach out to other people in order to make *contact* with them then friendship begins. Life passes from one to the other. Our love warms the coldness of the other person and brings them to life. Michelangelo's painting in the Sistine Chapel in Rome shows the creation of man, by God reaching out to man so that the tips of their fingers meet. Every beginning of friendship is a creation.

God wants our lives to be warmed by love and friendship. That is why he sent Jesus, who said he would not call us servants but friends. Jesus'

2

friendship is available to everyone. He is aware of our loneliness, yet respects our freedom. He stands before the closed door of our lives. 'I stand at the door and knock', he says, 'If anyone hears my voice and opens the door I will go in and we will have a meal together.'

In the depths of their being, lonely people hear the call but they are afraid; afraid of the consequence. If they never have had any friends, then why should God's Son want to be their friend now? But that surely is the point of the Christian faith. God loves us even when we don't love ourselves. Friendship begins not with our love for him but his love for us. His love heals our wounds and teaches us how to love and live.

Friendship is the great healer of wounds. When we reach out to one another in friendship then we come closest to God in creation. Jesus says to each one of us, 'I want to be your friend with no strings attached. It does not matter what you do or have done. My friendship is unconditional for you as a person. I shall always be there whether you need me or not. I want to be your friend and see you live a life full of love and happiness.' Jesus offers each one of us the hand of friendship. Don't refuse it and walk away into loneliness. Take it in your hand, feel its warmth and know you have a friend for life.

Lord Jesus, as we who are fortunate praise and thank you for our families and all who have taught us the value of friendship and encouraged us to make true friends in our journey through life, let us not be unmindful of those who are so locked up in themselves that they are unable to make friends. Bless those for whom today will be like yesterday, with no one to contact them or tell them that they need their friendship. Open our minds and hearts so that we may be sensitive to the deep longing of their hearts for the friendship they cannot express in words.

Hospitality

Jesus came to the Samaritan town called Sychar. Tired by the journey he sat straight down by the well. It was about the sixth hour, when a Samaritan woman came to draw water, Jesus said to her, 'Give me a drink.' (John 4: 5–7)

A meal shared with someone at a very special time can become a turning-point in our lives. Do you remember in the Bible how the two disciples ran away from Jerusalem in despair, because of the crucifixion and death of their master, and how they returned full of joy and hope once they had shared a meal with Jesus? In the breaking of bread they recognized him as their Risen Lord. Even a cup of water given to someone who is thirsty can dramatically alter situations and attitudes. The woman by Jacob's well gave Jesus a cup of water, and after he spoke to her her whole life was changed.

I remember one occasion when I asked a stranger for a glass of water, and the result certainly affected my attitude and my life. Let me tell you how it happened. In my early twenties I was sent by my bishop to Rome to study for the priesthood. What I did not know was that I would not be allowed to

5

return home for four years – not until I was ordained, made a priest. It was a shock to my system. It meant a complete change of lifestyle for me, as I had never lived abroad before. I didn't take too kindly to my new country or its people. I found that they were noisy, too extrovert, and talked too much, especially with their hands. The various types of pasta could never compare with the home cooking which I loved. All in all I was homesick, and was ready several times to ask the Superior for a single ticket home!

Then Easter came. It was a college custom for the students to travel, in groups of three, to various parts of Italy, so that we could get to know the people and the country. We received a college allowance of £15, which was to pay for rail fares, food, etc. for seven days. To call our adventure a holiday was a gross distortion of the truth. After four days the three of us were spent up, and exhausted. Since we were only fifty miles from Rome we decided to walk back home. It was a scorching hot day, and we were tired. As we were passing a farm house, the farmer saluted us. I mumbled a few Italian words and made gestures, pointing to my mouth, which would convey to anyone that I needed a drink of water. He replied – I only discovered this later – 'No one gets just a drink of water at my home. Come and join my family for a meal.' My goodness, what a meal it was! I never tasted spaghetti like it, the bread and cheese washed down with wine made us feel that it was good to be alive, to be young and – yes – to be living in Italy.

6

We were about to continue on our journey, when he insisted that we stay with him and his family for the rest of what had now become our holiday. He introduced us to all his friends, and we had the time of our lives. When we returned to Rome we were changed; I know I was. I love Italy and the Italians. The experience whetted my appetite for travelling abroad and getting to know the people and their customs.

The following Easter, our new-found friends Guiseppe and Maria – these were their names – and the family, came to Rome, which they had never visited before. We had a wonderful time together. Our time with them had changed us all, and I have remained their friend ever since. All because I asked for a glass of water.

Jesus compared heaven to a banquet where we all share a meal together in his Father's house. He also said that a glass of water given in his name would not go unrewarded. I think I know now, a little more clearly, what he meant. St Paul said that as Christians we were to make hospitality our special care. Hospitality opens up a whole new world of friendship, generosity and sharing.

Lord Jesus, when you lived in our world you fed the hungry in the desert and told your apostles that it was their duty to look after those who were hungry. In thanking you for our food and the shelter of our home, put a mind and heart in us that the stranger will always find a welcome at our door and a place at our table, because in welcoming him we will be welcoming you.

Roots

He came to Nazareth, where he had been brought up, and went into the synagogue on the sabbath day as he usually did. (Luke 4: 16)

Unless our childhood memories are unhappy we like at some time in our lives to go back to our roots. To visit again the place in which we were born or grew up. To breathe and live again the days of our youth. Because he was human, Jesus did just that. As soon as he began his public ministry the first place he headed for was Nazara, his own home town, where he was a carpenter. He went into the synagogue, and there for the first time he read the scripture lesson. Luke's gospel says that 'all eyes in the synagogue were fixed on him'. The grown man had come back to his own people.

Two years ago I decided to return to my roots, to my mother's home, in a remote part of County Cork. I hadn't been there since I was five. I had often passed nearby but somehow or other I never actually visited the place. I suppose I was afraid it would be so changed that all my dreams would be shattered, or that no one would remember me or my family. So I arranged to say Mass in the local church for the people one Sunday morning. To my surprise the church was packed with neighbours from the countryside around who remembered my mother and her family with genuine affection. This touched me deeply. Time had not changed them at all. They spoke about my mother, Margaret, as if she had left there only yesterday. She was part of them, their culture and heritage. They showed me where she went to school. It is still the same today – one classroom with one teacher for all the children, a typical village school.

Then my rediscovered friends took me to what had been my grandparents' farm. It took little imagination for me to see again my grandmother at the turf fire telling us all the folklore about the region as she puffed contentedly on her pipe, which she always held upside down. I found out only then that she never spoke a word of English, only Irish. And yet I could understand her quite easily, even at the age of three when I stayed at her farmhouse.

I looked over the land where once I played, or walked with my uncle behind the plough. There in the centre of the field was a circle of untilled land called the Fairy Ring. It was a raised mound of earth that was not to be disturbed by the plough, because otherwise the fairies would be angry and terrible things would happen! I remember as a child being intrigued and frightened by it. Children who live there today are still told the same fairy-stories. Time has stood still in my mother's homeland. Only we who once were children have grown old.

So for me the rediscovery of my roots was a happy occasion. I wonder what you remember about your roots. The street in which you played, your friends at school, the characters in your neighbourhood, the exciting adventurous things you did. The happy carefree times.

But perhaps your childhood was not very happy. If so, you may want to block out any recollection of your roots, because your memories of it are sad, even bitter, and have left their mark on you. I can appreciate that, and it grieves me when young children are treated so badly. And yet your roots are all part of you.

Your surroundings may not have been rich, but they held for you as for many of us a different wealth all of their own. Nazara was a broken-down, rather ramshackle village, so that people used to say, 'What good could come out of Nazareth?' Well Jesus did, and he wasn't ashamed or unhappy to go back to his roots.

Father, may those of us who give you thanks for our parents, brothers, sisters, friends, who helped us to grow up in a loving atmosphere, be mindful of those whose unhappy childhood still hurts them. Grateful for our own good fortune, may we pray that they be released from their hurtful memories so that in their lives they may bring glory to you who are the loving Father of us all.

Bereavement

We want you to be quite certain about those who have died, to make sure that you do not grieve about them, like the other people who have no hope. We believe that Jesus died and rose again, and that it will be the same for those who have died in Jesus. (1 Thessalonians 4: 13–14)

Every year I attend a very big conference on Inner Healing. People come for all parts of the country and beyond to share their experiences, their hopes and their fears. We all feel, and are, part of an extended family. And every year someone stands out as the 'star' of the conference, not so much for what they say but for what they are. Last year it was Sheila who was dying of cancer. This year it was her husband Richard. Their story is one of hope for us all. Let me share it with you.

Sheila and Richard were married fifteen years ago. Both outgoing, cheerful people, they were blessed with three beautiful boys, the eldest two being twins. Within a year of the birth of their youngest child Sheila developed a very severe form of cancer. She carried on bravely and lived life to the full, as best she could, for the next eleven years.

The boys always knew that their mother was 'not very well', but they never expected her to die. She did her best to prepare them and Richard for the day when she would no longer be physically with them.

But when she died the boys just couldn't make out what had happened. After all they were only thirteen and twelve. They always expected her to carry on not being well, but not to die. Richard was devastated. He just could not accept her death. He drew away from everyone and crept into his shell. His heart was not in his work, and every day was a long haul. Life went on around him, but he was dead inside. He was unable to share with anyone, least of all with the boys.

He told me, 'You don't know what it was like. At the end of the day I helped the boys with their homework and saw them off to bed. Then about 9.30 I sat down in my chair alone. It was the time of the day Sheila and I always shared together. It was so hellishly lonely that I often shouted at God in anger for letting it all happen. I felt I was living in a cage which I did not want anyone to enter. I was hurt and no one could heal me. I knew I was dying inside but I couldn't seem to pull myself out of the dark pit into which I had fallen.'

Richard started going downhill in his health. In his heart he knew that Sheila wouldn't want him to carry on like this. She loved El Shaddai and our work, and was very close to us. Richard made a final effort and came with his three sons to spend a day with us. He knew that Sheila found her peace

12

here just before she died. He wanted to experience that peace for himself and his sons. In the afternoon he stretched himself out on the lawn and fell asleep. During that sleep it was as if all the pain of her illness and the long weary months since her death were being soothed away. When he awoke he was a different person. For the first time he could feel her presence near him. The tears flowed and he was released from the cage he had built for himself. His sons who were playing at the other end of the lawn knew that something special had happened to their father. From that moment onwards a new and close relationship began between Richard and his sons. They sensed that he was free and that their mother was very close to him.

Now Richard knows that Sheila's love went beyond her own family and that its warmth reached out to many more people who needed her compassion and understanding. She healed people not so much by the way she bore her suffering, as by her joy in living. Richard and the boys are coming back to El Shaddai this summer. Like Sheila they are part of us and we are part of them. We all need each other, especially in times of sadness. But when we have walked through the valley into the sunlight, then perhaps we know we are never alone again. The ones we loved and lost a while are sharing the sunlight with us.

Lord Jesus, lover of life, who died and rose again so that we might be comforted at the death of a loved one, be with all those who today are bereaved and whose lives are drastically changed by death of a loved one. Help them to see beyond the grave to the brightness of new life and grant that one day they will be reunited with their loved one in heaven, where there will be no more mourning or weeping but only the happiness of everlasting life together.

Handicapped Children

'Let the children come to me; do not stop them; for it is to such as these that the kingdom of God belongs.' Then he put his arms around them, laid his hands on them, and gave them his blessing. (Mark 10: 14, 16)

Olivia is a very special person. Many people have come to know and love her. You see she has changed their lives, and brought out the best in them. And all this at the tender age of six and a half. What's so special about Olivia which has affected people so deeply? Let me tell you about her.

Olivia was a normal, happy, quite beautiful baby, and her parents, Margaret and Derrick, loved her dearly. Then at the age of two, Olivia contracted a strange virus, and a scan revealed that her brain was massively damaged. She could no longer speak, had no movement in her body, but worst of all she was blind. Her parents were shattered. It seemed like a horrible nightmare which they hoped would just go away. But Derrick, a very dedicated doctor, knew that there was no hope that she would ever recover, or even improve.

Margaret said, 'It broke our hearts to see our

15

lovely Olivia lying there so helpless and so lifeless. What affected us most was the fact that she could not see. We lived in the past, and remembered her before the virus struck her down. We could see nothing positive emerging from the tragedy.'

Fortunately she was wrong. A year later Derrick and Margaret brought Olivia to one of our healing services. There they experienced the love and hope of parents round them whose children, like Olivia, were also severely handicapped. Through that service their attitude towards Olivia began to change. Handicapped though she was, she was still their daughter. She needed to be loved, and love her they did.

And what a transformation happened! Olivia could sense the new dimension flowing into her life. She started to move her head, and then the rest of her body. Two years ago Olivia smiled for the first time since her illness. Her smile lights up her whole face. And that smile, despite her crippling handicaps, has won the hearts and minds of the many friends of the family who visit her home. Olivia seems so happy that it rubs off on everyone who comes in contact with her.

Her sister Elisha, aged seven, and her brother Peter, aged five, often lie next to her on her bean-bag, and they give her a big hug when they get back from school and tell her everything that has happened to them. Olivia seems to love it all. Both children know that she is very much their sister and part of a loving family. Wherever they go on their holidays or days out, Olivia goes too in the special family Land-rover built to meet her needs.

Margaret and Derrick face the future now with great hope. Of course they would love Olivia to see again, but they leave it all in the hands of God. He has helped them up to now to bear the burden. And they believe that he will be with them in the future. They love their daughter, and they know that this is the most precious gift that they can give her. The whole family has grown together in a beautifully sensitive way. There is real laughter in their home, and they act like any normal, caring, sharing family.

Even now, Margaret and Derrick cannot understand why it happened to their daughter. But it has, and they know they have to get on with living their lives. Jesus said of little children that they are close to the kingdom of heaven. It is certainly true of Olivia. I have her photograph on my mantelpiece. From it she smiles down at me to brighten up my day. For her and all handicapped children and their parents, I say a quiet prayer every day that together they may share in the love that heals and draws us closer together.

Lord Jesus, you had a special love for children, I ask you to bless and heal with your peace all those who are blind and cannot see the beauty of our world or the faces of their parents; those who suffer from brain damage and cannot join in the conversation and activity of those around them; those who are deaf and cannot speak or must lie in bed while other children play games and enjoy the pleasures of life. Bless also the parents and those who have care of them, and may they be helped by the sure knowledge that in their love they are ministering to a wounded Christ.

Good News

I have told you this so that my own joy be in you and your joy be complete. (John 15: 11)

A happy person is one who brings good news, someone who is a sign of hope to other people. Jesus was the happiest person who ever lived. Happy people experience disappointments in their lives. Their friends may melt away in time of crisis, and sometimes they seem to be standing alone for what they believe in. But they are never cast down for long. Pope John Paul says there is no such person as a gloomy Christian.

I know lots of happy people; some of them are Christian and some are not. I think the example of Jimmy will help us all. He is parish priest of one of the most depressed areas in Liverpool. By temperament, he is, I suppose, a happy person. But there is more to him than that. No matter what difficulties he faces daily, he always seems to rise above them. A smile is never far from his lips, and the sound of laughter is in his voice. He thinks we are living in exciting times, and that it's great to be alive. No one can be happy twenty-fours hours a day. Father

Jimmy knows that only too well. I know that too. Often the people you pin your hopes on let you down. Father Jimmy was for years a fervent supporter of young people, and gave them a great deal of his time, but then in the 'seventies they seemed to go berserk. They broke into people's houses, terrorized the old people, and soon the area was a very violent one. But Father Jimmy couldn't sit back and let these things happen. He sent his young assistant, Duncan, to share in the life of the young people on the streets. Duncan soon realized that the young people saw life as a video game in which they were disposable pawns. They were no-hopers, and bad news was all they heard.

Gradually the situation was diffused because Father Jimmy and others gave the young people something to hope for in the way of jobs and housing. The area which might have gone up in flames, like Toxteth, settled down. But youth will be youth, and they are no angels. 'Occasionally', says Father Jimmy with a big grin and an understanding shrug of his shoulders, 'they play football in the streets at two o'clock in the morning, but at least they are not breaking into houses.'

You and I may be surrounded by bad news coming at us from all sides, and we may be tempted to say, 'What the heck!' We may even join the moaners. But remember today is a new day. Look for the *good* news and spread it around. Father Jimmy doesn't pack his church on Sundays. It's not that kind of place, and they are not that kind of people. But to everyone in the surrounding estates

Father Jimmy is one of them. They smother him with their problems. 'At least', he says, 'they know where to come to.' Sometimes his parishioners let him down badly, and he feels it deep inside. But he knows that that's life. When some of them turn out well, he considers that a bonus. 'If they succeed here,' he says, 'they will succeed anywhere.'

So Father Jimmy carries on bringing good news to the people he loves. He makes the Gospel come alive for them. 'I have come', said Jesus, 'to bring the good news to the poor.' He brings that good news to you and me. Today you may feel depressed and beaten. You may think that things have got beyond you, and you can't cope. Be patient with yourself. The mists will clear and you will find a way out of your present crisis. God is near – nearer than you think, and he wants you to be happy. There are Father Jimmys in your world. Go to them. They are people of hope for you and me. They are the ones with the really good news.

Lord Jesus, you brought joy into this world and into the lives of so many people. You shared your joy with everyone: with shepherds at your birth, with the guests at the wedding feast in Cana who drank your very special wine, with the children who clung to you, the lepers who cried out to you, with the people who crowded round you everywhere to listen to your message of hope, with Mary your mother, whom you loved more than anyone and with whom you shared your life. We thank you that this joy was not destroyed by your death but came renewed into our world by your resurrection. May the light of your joy shine through me today so that I may reflect it to those around me and lift them up in hope and joy.

Nostalgia

I will not leave you orphans; I will come back to you. Do not let your hearts be troubled or afraid. (John 14: 18, 27)

We all like to have a good old grumble sometimes about the sad state of the world today. 'It is going to the dogs,' we say, or 'People wouldn't have done that in my day.' Yes, 'things ain't what they used to be.' I suppose it is a way of letting off steam. But for some people it is more serious than that. They see little or no good in the present world, mainly because they have idealized the past. They still live in it.

Looking back on the past is a bad thing if it freezes us in a moment of time, so that we are unable to move forward into the present. It is like a still in a movie-film, or a record which gets caught in the groove. There is no movement, no ongoing melody. If we are people like that, then, to put it generously, we are pessimists who need large doses of joy, humour, and a spirit of adventure. The medicine is called 'life' and it doesn't taste as bad as the pessimists say it does.

In a sense it is good to indulge in a little bit of

nostalgia now and then. It is a luxury we should all be able to afford. I often think back to my father, and the character he was. He used to keep us enthralled with stories on many a winter's evening as we sat around the kitchen fire with all the lights out. He was a born story-teller, and he loved a captive audience as he unfolded his story in a hushed, dramatic voice. Even though he had a very strong, reliable character, he was a child at heart. I suppose that is why, when he took me to the sea-side to fly my new kite we had been making for weeks, it was he who flew it all day. He was so mesmerized by it. I ran off crying to my mother because I never 'got a go'. He laughingly taught me how, and we then shared the joy together. It was the same with my train set. He was always getting me new pieces for it but he was station master, driver, porter and passenger. Eventually I 'caught' his enthusiasm and his zest for living. He taught me the secret of staying young at heart.

And yet, on hindsight, I can see that his life was never easy. He knew sadness, disappointments, and he grew through them all. My mother died when I was fourteen and I saw him wobble then, but he picked up the pieces because he had to for our sake. His business fell apart in the war years, and it grieved him that our standard of living took a terrible battering. The troubles in Northern Ireland often moved him to tears, and ultimately to the sadness of silence. And yet to the end he had an overriding sense of humour which invariably bub-bled to the top. His time was the day he was living in, and he lived life to the full. If anyone was alive and a Christian he was.

As Christians we are often accused of living in the past. But if Christianity is not about present-day life and living it fully, then it is meaningless escapism. Jesus used the past, and all the traditions of his Jewish ancestors, to make his listeners aware of what life was all about. He wanted them to read the signs of the times. He said we should not worry about tomorrow, and were to 'leave the dead to bury the dead'. Each day has enough troubles of its own. Not that today's world is any better or worse than yesterday's. But I'm glad I've known the past with its sweet memories. It helps me to live the present moment to the full.

Father, from whom all fatherhood on earth comes, I give you thanks for my father and the hours of my childhood which he spent lovingly with me. I pray that you will bless those less fortunate than myself who have never known a father's love, and give them the grace to be the kind of parent to their children that they would have longed to have known themselves.

Working in Hope

Now be patient, brothers, until the Lord's coming. Think of a farmer; how patiently he waits for the precious fruit of the ground until it has had the autumn rains and the spring rains! You too have to be patient. Do not lose heart, because the Lord's coming will be soon. (James 5: 7–8)

As I write these words, spring is in the air. My garden at the moment is bursting with life. Daffodils are everywhere. It has made all the back-breaking work seem worthwhile. Then the soil seemed dead and unyielding, but today there are green shoots of new life everywhere. Spring is the time of new life, of hope.

I want to tell you a story about hope and how in our work we must be patient to see the fruits of our labour. It concerns Jim. He was a farmer and his holding, though small, was everything a farm should be, and his two sons shared his love for the soil. They were a joy to know. I became very friendly with the family, and spent many a happy evening with them. Jim and I shared a lot in common.

Then tragedy struck. In late summer, when they

were busy gathering in the harvest, Jim took ill suddenly and was rushed to hospital. He was diagnosed as having a severe form of cancer and a life expectancy of six months. Everyone was shocked. He had always been robustly healthy, and was only in his early fifties. But, true to form, he carried on as if nothing had happened, and was soon back on the land with his sons, ploughing, harrowing and preparing for the next year's harvest.

Shortly after Christmas his condition deteriorated, and he was confined to his home where I visited regularly. He hung on to life with grim determination, but it was obvious the end was near. One morning I called round to see him at his home, but his wife told me that he had insisted on one of his sons dressing him and taking him in the Land Rover round the farm. I went in search of him, and eventually found him wrapped in blankets, sitting in the Land Rover looking proudly out over his land. 'I've ploughed it and sown the seed,' he said, 'and I just wanted to see the green shoots above the ground. Aye, the seed has taken well. It'll be a good harvest this year.' Jim died four days later. His sons harvested what Jim had worked and sown in hope.

In life there are many things we do which will not come to fulfilment in our lifetime, but we do them just the same because we believe, we hope, that others will reap the rewards of our labours. One man sows, another man reaps. Jesus gave his life so that we might have everlasting life. He sowed, we reap. We are the green shoots of the new Christian life. His death and resurrection is our hope. He gives meaning to those things we are not able to finish in our lifetime. He will take care that our work will not be in vain. It is sufficient that we have sown; we leave the end result, the harvest, to God. He knows what he is about. We will not allow the ground to grow fallow because we are ill or have grown old. We will continue our work knowing and believing that God will increase what we have done a hundredfold, even though we may never see it during our time on earth.

Father, since you do nothing in vain and all things are for our good, give me a mind at peace and a heart at rest which trusts you in all my undertakings so that, though I may never see the end-result of my labours, I am confident they will come to a successful conclusion through your wisdom, power and love.

My New Pet

Look at the birds in the sky. They do not sow, or reap, or gather into barns; yet your heavenly Father feeds them. (Matthew 6: 26)

Animals are God's gift to us. And we should treat such a gift with respect and sensitivity. If we have a correct attitude to animals then we will grow as human beings, and the world will be a better place. Animals are an essential part of the wonder of creation and contribute so much to the quality of our lives. Ever since I was a child, dogs have been part of my life. Wherever or whenever possible I have had a dog as a pet or companion. They were all special with their own individual characteristics, and I loved them all. But my favourite was Pax, my red setter, not because she had twenty-two puppies in one litter and found her place in the *Guinness Book of Records*, but because she shared twelve years of the most challenging period in my life. When I buried her in the presbytery garden I felt I was burying part of me. She had been a constant and loyal companion who seemed to sense my every mood. I was so lonely I decided that I would never have another dog again. No other dog would or could take Pax's place.

Time is a great healer. I needed a dog, even though I wouldn't admit it to myself. After a suitable interval my friends began to suggest that I might have a puppy. A special friend went further. He invited me to his home for dinner. After a very good meal he told me he had a very pleasant surprise for me. He brought me into a room where his beautiful red setter was nursing her litter of pups. It brought back memories of Pax and her pups. 'Now Michael,' said my friend, 'what about it? Wouldn't you like to have one of these? I want you to have first choice!' As I lifted a little pup and nestled her in the palm of one hand, my heart melted. I immediately called her Pax.

Weeks later when little Pax was able to leave her mother, my friend brought her to her new home, the presbytery. Within days my house was turned upside down. Carpets and cushions were chewed, newspapers were torn into a thousand pieces, legs of chairs were used as ideal material to sharpen teeth, until my study looked as if it had been invaded by a marauding gang of house-breakers. Her favourite pastime was to leave little messages everywhere in the most unexpected and unwelcome places. Whenever I opened the front door I expected the worst. Pax never failed to surprise and horrify me. She was a beautiful, happy creature, but what a menace. Many times on Sunday, at the most solemn moments of the Mass, she managed to slip into the sanctuary, much to my confusion and the delight of the parishioners, whom she generously greeted with the 'lick of peace'. My goodness, what had I taken on?

I hadn't the time to train her myself, so I sent her off on a six-weeks crash course in obedience and house-training. While she was away I realized how much I missed her. The house seemed so orderly and so lonely. She came back a reformed character, responding to my every call and instruction. Pax was trained but free. Now we could become real pals with all fear of a wrecked home forever removed.

A few years ago we moved to the country, just five miles from the sea. Pax loves her new home. She jumps the wooden fence into the field as beautifully as Arkle and chases rabbits she can never catch. She enlarges a few of their burrows so that only her tail is above the ground, like a periscope. The sea is her great thrill, and she acts as excitedly as any child, chasing seagulls, sand martins and anything that will fly because she doesn't like to see them just standing there idly on the sand. In the house she turns the handles of the door with her teeth until she finds company. The new Pax has helped to heal me of many wounds from former years and I wouldn't be without her.

I know that human friendship is God's most precious gift to us. But animals are his special gift too in their own way. Pax offers me so much that I treasure in loyalty and companionship. She seems to sense my every mood and never lets me forget that she is always near whenever I need her. Her boundless energy keeps me young. Whenever I take her out for a walk she makes me feel it is good to be alive, because her enthusiasm for life is infectious. Through her I make many new friends. Who can resist a red setter who runs up to you and refuses to stop wagging her tail until you acknowledge her presence? Yes, I thank God that he gave us animals to share our world. I'm glad that he gave me such a loyal companion and gift as Pax.

Yes, animals are beautiful. Jesus rode on a donkey for his triumphal entry into Jerusalem. By this he showed his love and need of animals. May we never use animals cruelly or as mere beasts of burden. I am sure God meant us to have pets and to value their service and companionship. They are part of his glorious creation in which we see his loving hand at work. We thank him for animals, for their companionship, their loyalty, and for all the joy they bring into our lives.

God, loving creator of all life, help us to be grateful for the companionship of animals. May we treat them with compassion, as gifts from you entrusted to our care, and never subject them to cruelty or neglect. May the charge you give us over them be a partnership of mutual service, so that through them we may come to a greater appreciation of your glory in creation.

Follow Your Star

And there in front of them was the star they had seen rising; it went forward and halted over the place where the child Jesus was. (Matthew 2: 9)

Do you remember the story of Epiphany? It is all about three kings or wise men – call them what you like – who saw a very special star in the sky, and followed it across the desert. They believed it had a meaning and a message for them. They saw it as a sign that a great new age was going to begin in the world, that a new, powerful king had been born. They wanted to be there to witness it, and to share in it. And sure enough the star led them to Jerusalem, the ancient capital of the Jews. Here was surely the journey's end for them. This was obviously where the star wanted them to be. And so excitedly they asked everyone, 'Where is the new king?'

But their question caused amusement, if not derision, among the people of Jerusalem. They already had a king, Herod, and if these strange eastern folk were talking about the 'Messiah', then they knew all about him from the books of the prophets, and didn't need to do such a foolish thing as to follow the star across a desert.

Eventually the strangers were brought to Herod who, in the words of another monarch, 'was not amused'. To put it mildly, the wise men were 'laughed out of court'. Soon they left Jerusalem: I presume they were pretty disillusioned with what they found there. Was the star wrong or were the people of Jerusalem, from the king downwards, too smug?

When the strangers saw the star again beyond Jerusalem they had to make a fresh decision, a recommitment to their belief, that the star still had a message for them. The rest of their journey might be brief, but the heart-searching within them must have been long and painstaking. What tipped the scales we will never know. But they did journey on. They did follow the star to the journey's end. They found their king, not in a palace, but in a humble stable where even the homeless would feel at home.

They left their gifts for him, and in the process found a peace that no one in Jerusalem knew existed. They had followed their star. They did it because deep within themselves they had to do it if they were to find fulfilment within themselves. They returned to their country praising their God their way because they had found something very precious which made their life and journey worth while.

Each of us needs a star to guide our lives. We ask ourselves the questions: What is my star and what price am I prepared to pay for following it? Or have

I given up the search because of the disappointments I have met on the way? Do I have to look for my star? Not in the sky but within myself. What do I want to do most with my life?

I know where my star is. It has always been the same, even though at times it gets a little dim. I want to be myself, and as myself I want to bring inner peace to others. In the process I find peace myself. Thank God for the stars, and for people who follow them right to the journey's end whatever the cost.

Father, by a star you led the wise men to the place where your Son was to be found; help us to follow the star in our lives so that, even though its brightness and presence may often be hidden from our eyes, we will know by faith it is still there leading us closer each day to finding Christ in every step of our journey.

Communication

They went as far as Capernaum, and as soon as the sabbath came he went to the synagogue and began to teach. And his teaching made a deep impression on them because, unlike the scribes, he taught them with authority. (Mark 1: 21–2)

We live in a very exciting age and world, and I have great hopes for the future. One of the main reasons for my optimism is the wonderful advances that are being made in communication. Communication has always fascinated me, and I am very fortunate that I have been so involved in it for the greater part of my life. And, my goodness, what startling changes have taken place during my lifetime!

I remember quite clearly, as a very young child, the first time I ever heard a recorded voice. It was on a gramophone. The gramophone, called 'His Master's Voice', was my father's newest and most treasured possession. When he first brought it home we were all made to sit quietly on the floor of the drawing room as he wound the handle and put the record on. We were entranced as we heard the voice of Ireland's greatest tenor, John McCormack, sing-ing one of my mother's favourite songs, 'The Rose of Tralee'. When the record was finished there was a hush in the room. Then bedlam broke loose as we wanted to know if it was really ours, and how it worked. We thought my father was a magician. I think he kind of liked that.

He loved sharing, and showing off a bit. So one weekend he brought the gramophone to my granny's house in the country. And all the neighbours from round about came flocking in to hear this wonderful new invention. They filled the house, sitting on the stairs, and even out through the door into the garden. Then they heard John McCormack sing. They were as spellbound as we had been. They made my father play the record over and over again. The gramophone opened up a whole new world to them, and I was proud that it was my father who was the one who made it possible.

How communication has changed since then. Today we live in the satellite age. Our world has shrunk to the size of a village. News has always been news, but satellite television has made it almost instant news. An important event in Peking or Peru will be flashed on our screens within minutes, even seconds, of it happening. Satellite television, as never before, can help us to be aware more quickly of how we can come to the aid of those suffering from famine or a national disaster.

The possibilities for good are endless, and that is how I look at the modern developments in communication – positively, not negatively. They shed new light on the words of the Bible, 'Nation shall speak peace to nation.'

And how do the developments in communication affect the Gospel of Jesus Christ? Basically the message has not changed, even though the method of presentation has taken on other dimensions. The message is still simple. Jesus spoke to people's hearts. He knew that they were hungry for a meaning to life. His was the message they longed to hear. They instinctively sensed that he was different from other preachers because his life and his words were as one. He was completely genuine. However large the crowd, they felt that he was speaking to them personally, one to one. And that is why they flocked to hear him wherever he went.

So whatever the medium, we let him speak through us by being completely sincere. We speak to people as in a one to one situation. What is really important is that, through us, people hear the good news of a loving God who cares for them, because he loves them.

Lord, today people will be communicating to us through books, papers, radio and television; people will be talking to us in a hundred and one different ways. Help us to listen, so that everything we read or see may be through your eyes, everything we hear may be through your ears, and all that is happening in the world round us may affect our whole person which we pray will be at one with you. Send your Spirit to be with us when we speak so that our message may be of the good news of your life for each one of us and the world in which we live.

Vision

Jesus took the blind man by the hand and led him outside the village. Then he laid his hands on the man's eyes and he saw clearly. (Mark 8: 23, 25)

Martin is a very courageous, resourceful young Irish man. He wouldn't take it being unemployed, so one morning without a word to anyone he set off on his own for Dublin. This in itself was a great adventure as he had never been outside his own village. From Dublin, he took the ferry to England, and ended up in London in the early hours of the morning. He had just one contact in the city, the name of his cousin, but no address. It was a very common Irish name, filling over eight pages of the telephone directory, but using a public call box, Martin, through a girl he met on the train, resolutely dialled the numbers one by one until he came to his cousin's number. Then he got a taxi and landed up on Pat's doorstep. 'I've come for work,' he said.

What's so resourceful about that? Well, Martin had been blind from the age of four, and he set out on this long journey all on his own because he wanted to get work, to do something useful with his life. He loved life and felt that London was the place for him. That was where he landed up, and where he lives happily today. He was helped at every stage of his journey by people whom he had never met before and without whom he would have never reached his destination. This made such an impact on him at a very impressionable time in his life that he always talks of the innate goodness of people and, whenever he can, he does his best to help people himself. This attitude has made him a lot of friends in this country.

It was some of these friends who told me all about him. And knowing that I was involved in the ministry of healing, they asked me if I would pray that he might see. They felt in a sense that because he was so brave he deserved it. So they brought him to me, and I found him full of laughter and apparently happy. I could hardly believe the things he was able to do even though he was blind. I asked him what he wanted me to pray for. 'God will tell you,' he said. I could feel the tangible presence of God round us like a gentle cloud, and then I knew what I was meant to do, and for what I should pray. I waited a few minutes before doing anything. I laid my hands gently on his head, not on his eyes, and prayed for his inner peace of soul. I knew God was in that prayer and touch as I watched the peace of Christ flood Martin's face. He was happy before. Now he was aglow. This is what he told me afterwards.

'For years I have been to healing sessions and, every time, the people who want to heal me touch my eyes and ask for the gift of sight for me. What I have really craved for all these years was inner peace of mind and soul, but no one prayed for that. I have been aware for years, not of my lack of sight, but the lack of the deep presence of God, and of his peace. When I felt the touch of your hands it was like a new life, and my soul was flooded with a peace I have never experienced before. People think I resent my blindness. They are wrong. I'm used to being blind, but I need that inner peace so that I can be aware of myself as a whole person.'

So, this resourceful young man, though blind, travelled hundreds of miles on his own in search of work. And although he was apparently happy, he wanted something more than the obvious. Like the paralytic in the gospel story who desired more than just the power to walk, he wanted to be at deep peace with God. Martin, resourceful though he was, knew that the peace he sought would come from a deeper source, one that would give him an inner vision, and light him up from within so that, though blind, he could look at life in a new way.

We should never be afraid to ask God for deep inner peace of soul. It is the one gift he will always give us because it is the important gift we need if we are to be truly happy on the inside. Today, amid all the bustle and upsets that the day will bring, just close your eyes for a moment and allow God to touch you with his peace. If you remain still in your body and mind, you will know that his peace for which you long is already deep inside you, before the words are on your lips. May your eyes be opened to God's peace in the world around you, because what you see reflects what you are experiencing deep within you.

Father, your Son Jesus gave to those who pleaded for healing more than they asked for. He touched their skin and healed the deep wounds of the spirit. May we be touched by the same healing power and thus be released from the hidden forces deep within us which hold us back from true health of mind and body. May the peace within us shed its light and warmth on all those around us. Give to us the eyes of faith so that we may see your love and peace at work within us.

Budgies and Eagles

Young men may grow tired and weary, youths may stumble, but those who hope in God renew their strength, they put out wings like eagles. They run and do not grow weary, walk and never tire. (Isaiah 40: 30–1)

One of my favourite sayings is 'Don't be a budgie, be an eagle'. Budgies are restricted to flying within their small cage, whereas an eagle soars through the air, wings outstretched, with the sky as its home. A story is told of a boy who stole a baby eagle from its nest and put it in a fairly big cage with budgies and other small birds. Grown up and cruelly confined within the cage, it saw an eagle soaring effortlessly through the air. 'Oh,' the eagle said, 'how I wish I could fly like that.' 'Nonsense,' said the budgie, 'only eagles fly like that. And you're just a budgie like us.' So the eagle lived and died in the cage never knowing that it was meant to soar freely through the air with the sky as its home.

The moral of the story is simple. God meant us to be eagles, not budgies. So don't allow yourself to be caged in by anyone or anything. Don't let anyone devalue your true worth in your eyes. Soar above their negative criticism. The sky is your home and not a cage. Be yourself. And yet so many people are budgies, even though we were meant to be free to fly like eagles. We are afraid to face the challenge outside the security of our cages – afraid to be different, afraid to fly. On the one hand we want to be free, with all the happiness this would give us, yet we shy away from the responsibility which such freedom involves. So we do not choose the cage so much as fail to be eagles by default. We are nervous of change, of what would happen when we stretch our wings. Would we fall? Would we miss the security of our former way of life? Yet without freedom we would not be human. It takes courage to fly and to be free. And there is a budgie and an eagle in each one of us.

Take St Peter for example. He was the leader of the apostles, the one who was commended by Jesus for his strong faith. Yet on the night before Jesus died he was afraid to be himself. He played the budgie in front of the Roman soldiers and a servant girl, and denied that he even knew Jesus. Then he went through a period of fear for a couple of months and was in hiding from the Jewish authorities. He and the other apostles were in their cage when the Holy Spirit came and gave them the courage to be different. They went out into the streets of Jerusalem and proclaimed to their astonished listeners, 'You killed Jesus but God raised him to life.' The budgies had become eagles, and the result of their message was astonishing. That very day about three thousand were added to their number.

This would never have happened if they had not chosen to dare to be different because of the message which penetrated their whole being. Jesus himself knew of this fear within people to soar above criticism and rejection by others. Jesus was a Jew and it saddened him that, even though he preached freedom from the beginning of his public life, his own people did not believe him. And yet there were some who did believe him, even among the leading men, but they did not admit it, through fear of the Pharisees and fear of being expelled from the synagogue. They put honour from men before the honour that comes from God. What a different story it would have been if they had had the courage to stand up and be counted for what they believed in.

Much of what is good in our lives never sees the light of day because of fear. We are frightened of what people will think of us. We are afraid of losing face. We are beaten in spirit, and we act like budgies making people happy, because this is the easiest way to live a 'peaceful' life. Yet there are situations all round the world when in the midst of the most frightening tortures and punishment people of conscience speak up for what they believe. They may be in prison but they are the ones who are truly free, because they are eagles.

The door of your cage is open. Why don't you leave it behind and face the challenge which the day may bring. You will feel better when you breathe the fresh air of freedom. Today is the time to learn to fly. If you begin to fall, the Lord will bear you up. Soon you will soar through the air with your wings outstretched and the sky as your home. And you will see your world from a new vantage point.

Father, you treat us as tenderly as an eagle who supports her young on her wings as they learn to fly. Be with us today and every day as we witness to your Son Jesus Christ, who gave his life as a testimony of his love for you and for us. May we never be afraid to proclaim your never-failing love, so that through our faith others may learn to believe.

Time and Space

When Christ freed us, he meant us to remain free. Stand firm, therefore, and do not submit again to the yoke of slavery. (Galatians 5: 1)

Freedom to grow, to be yourself, is the secret recipe for happiness. To do the things in life that help the real you to express itself. And for this you need *time and space*. But the world hems us in on all sides. It may be large, but for many their individual world is claustrophobic. I suppose it has always been so. Today so many people, threatened by collaterals and cholesterols, are shouting out deep inside themselves, 'Stop the world. I want to get off'.

It was really no different in the time of Jesus. Wherever he went the crowds followed him, begging for healing or grabbing him by his clothes. Whenever he visited a house, St Mark tells us in his gospel, 'the whole town came crowding round the door.' Not much time or space there for himself! Jesus knew that and made allowances for it. 'In the morning, long before dawn', continues St Mark, 'he got up and left the house, and went off to a lonely place and prayed there.' I don't expect many of you listening to me will be up before dawn tomorrow morning praying. But you and I and everyone need to have time and space in our lives to breathe – to relax and be ourselves, to live the kind of life that helps us to grow as individual persons.

The choice isn't always there for everyone. That's why the world can be such a cruel place. But many people who have the opportunity to grow put it aside, because they set their sights on wealth, power, prestige or fame to such an extent that they never have sufficient time for themselves or those they love. I could quote hundreds of cases of this form of pressure, but Michael is a typical example of what I mean.

Michael's educational background was slight, being one of those less enriched by the secondary modern system. But Michael was keen to succeed, had a very easy personal manner, and by his early thirties he was a highly successful businessman. He told me, 'I worked sometimes from six in the morning until eight in the evening to make money I didn't really need. I had reached the stage where I knew I would be comfortably off for the rest of my life. From then on I knew I was becoming greedy. I could see what was happening to me. At the weekend there would be as many as sixty phone calls. I had subconsciously allowed my business to invade my home. It was a terrible life. I hardly ever saw my children. My wife and I confined our social life to business contacts. So one day I decided to cut back. It was the best decision I ever made. Now I spend many happy hours with my wife and family.

I am fortunate enough to have the time and money to do the things I have always wanted to do. My health is much better, and my set of values has, I hope, changed for the better. I don't envy anyone, and I know deep inside me that there is more to life than living in a pressure-cooker atmosphere.'

So the moral for us all is to be found in the words of Jesus, 'Look at the birds of the air. They do not sow or reap or gather into barns; yet your heavenly Father feeds them.' God doesn't want us to be budgies living cramped up in a cage. He wants us to have the space and time which give us the freedom to fly like an eagle. So don't be a budgie. Be free like an eagle.

Jesus, you said that your mission was to set the prisoners free. We are prisoners locked in a cage of our own making and are too preoccupied with what the world calls success. We forget so easily that life means more than food and the body more than clothing, and that you have invited us to look at the birds in the air flying so gracefully and freely. They are fed by our Heavenly Father. Lord, fill us with the courage to walk freely from our self-made prison so that, given time and space, we may grow into the loving person you would have us be.

A Family of Friends

Be united in your love. There must be no competition among you, no conceit; but everybody is to be self-effacing. Always consider the other person to be better than yourself, so that nobody thinks of his own interest first, but everybody thinks of other people's interest instead. In your minds you must be the same as Christ Jesus. (Philippians 2: 2–5)

We all need people close to us with whom we can share our hopes and fears, our joys and sorrows, the deepest moments of our lives. That is why Jesus came on earth. He wants to share his life with us. 'Where two or three are gathered together in my name,' he said, 'I am there in the midst of them.' It is like being in a family of which Christ is a loving member.

When God created human beings he chose for us to live in a family setting. He intended members of every family to be friends, to love and share deeply with each other. As we know, it doesn't always work out that way, but when it does, then we witness and experience something beautiful. In my lifetime I have known hundreds of truly happy families who, through their love, have been real friends to each other. Margaret and John and their six children are such a family. I call them a family of friends. They really care deeply for each other. I have been very close to them for over twenty years, and have watched them grow into the kind of loving people they are today.

Each one of the family has had at least one fairly major crisis over the years. Who hasn't? (Even Jesus caused a crisis in his family when he stayed behind in the temple for a few days at the tender and unpredictable age of twelve.) The last crisis to hit Margaret and John and their family is still going on. As in other crises the whole family is rallying round. They are supporting Clare, the youngest in the family who, just before her final year at university, contracted the dread disease known as ME, myalgic encephalomyelitis. Previously she was an outgoing, outdoor type of girl, full of vitality and a great sportswoman. Her illness made her withdrawn, depressed, with little or no energy to do anything. In fact, suddenly she was no longer the kind of person whom the family had known and loved all her life.

Margaret is very honest in summing up their attitude to the present crisis. 'It affected us all. We just didn't know what was happening to our daughter. She was the last to leave the nest when this crisis came down like a cloud over her life. Thank God we found an excellent consultant who is helping us. The family was, and is, marvellous. But what really supported us all was our unshakeable belief that

God would see us through. This was the inner force that gave us hope.'

Today Clare is back at university after two and a half years at home. She is trying to pick up the pieces of her life again and meet the friends with whom she had lost contact during her illness. She will recover. She knows that not only has she the support of her family, but of Jesus himself. His promise, that he would help us if we were in trouble and were to come to him for peace and rest, is certainly true in her case. She has grown very close to the Lord during her illness. Her advice to anyone who is fighting to recover health and happiness in their lives, is to remember that we are not alone. We need a friend to help us, with whom we can share our worries. God does not want anyone to suffer alone. That is why he gave us his Son to walk with us as our friend. Jesus came on earth as one of the family. He suffered death and rose again. In his sharing in our sufferings we will share his resurrection.

Lord Jesus Christ, be with us as a family so that we may always have a great love for you. Make us gentle, courteous and loving towards each other; take from us all misunderstanding so that no angry or bitter word may cross our lips, and grant that we may treat each other as you treated those with whom you shared your human family. Keep us close to one another and lead us at last to our true and heavenly home.

Worry

Can any of you, for all your worrying, add one single day to your span of life? So do not worry about tomorrow; tomorrow will take care of itself. Each day has enough trouble of its own. (Matthew 6: 27, 34)

Stress causes ill health – I have always thought that. So I was not surprised when I read in a medical journal that over 30 per cent of illnesses today have their roots, in varying degrees, in stress and tension. This was the conclusion of an in-depth survey carried out over seven years by some of the world's top doctors, psychiatrists and those engaged in community medicine. Some diseases, they say, are particularly subject to stress. For example, 40 per cent of secondary cancer is attributable to stress. Many physical and emotional illnesses, which have only appeared in recent times, baffle doctors and psychiatrists. They cannot find a remedy, because basically they are unable to pin-point the cause. The human person is much more complex than a body or a mind.

The conclusion that we can draw from all this is that if we want to be whole, if we want to be healthy, then we must learn to relax and be at peace. Inner peace is essential for our health. Worry is the great destroyer of peace. A worried person is a divided person; he is at war with himself. Worry can take such a hold on us that it dominates our sleeping as well as our waking hours. Morning finds us tired, unable to cope with what the day may bring.

Mary is a typical example of someone who is torn apart by worry. From the moment she gets up in the morning she sees problems lurking everywhere and coming at her from all directions. She hates to open a letter, answer the 'phone, or meet somebody because they will only add to the tension. She wastes all her energy and her life expecting the worst and is surprised, even disappointed, when it does not happen. She thinks this only means that a bigger problem is in the offing. We have tried over the years to help Mary find peace of mind and heart, and so far we have only been moderately successful because basically, I think, she likes to feel surrounded by problems.

Her healing is not made any easier by the fact that she, like all of us, is caught up in a stress-filled world. Worry has taken the place of cholesterols as the menace to health. Many of our worries and fears are the product of the imagination. We often blow up our problems out of all proportion to reality. And so, if we want to be peaceful, we need to face reality.

All right, so we have some *real* problems to face which can make or break us. Physical or mental sickness in ourselves or in those we love can change a happy way of life. There's a death in the family or some financial upheaval which throws us right off balance. What do we do then? How can we solve these problems, cope with these stresses? One thing is certain. We will never solve them by worrying about them.

If we want to be at peace, then we need to share our worry with someone who will listen because they care about us. We need to talk. They need to listen. And together we can face the problem because we know we are no longer alone. Jesus wants us to share our burden with him. 'Come to me,' he said, 'all you who are heavily burdened and I will give you rest, give you peace.' He also said that worry does not add a single day to our span of life. In fact, worry shortens it. Jesus had problems too which he needed to share with others. The night before he died, he took his three closest friends Peter, James and John to be company for him as he prayed in the darkness of a garden. On the way to Calvary his cross was so heavy that he was grateful to Simon of Cyrene for helping to share his load. So we have to try to stop worrying and learn to share.

Slow me down, Lord.
Ease the pounding of my heart
by the quieting of my mind.
Teach me the art of slowing down
to look at a flower,

to chat to a friend,
to read a few lines from a good book.
Let me look upward into the branches of the towering oak
and know that it grew great and strong
because it grew slowly and well.

The Full Life

*Happy all those who love God. May God bless you from Zion
all the days of your life. May you see Jerusalem prosperous,
and live to see your children's children.* (Psalm 128: 1, 5–6)

I discovered for myself long ago that one of the
most important things in life is to live one day at a
time. To try to take each day with its ups and downs
and live it to the full. And who better to illustrate
this point than Arthur. Arthur has been a friend of
mine for over thirty-five years. Whenever I meet
him, as often as not, he has an infectious smile on
his face, which does my heart good to see. I would
call him a happy man – a man who is happy with
life because he lives life to the full, one day at a
time. Mind you he has not always found it easy.
He is a tailor whose eyesight has always given him
trouble since his teens, and then in his forties he
became nearly blind. 'What's the use of grumbling?'
he would say, 'I can still see to do my work and
that's good enough for me.' He built up a flourish-
ing business, but then the advent of casual wear
and the craze for jeans meant the virtual end of
lounge suits which were his real trade and craft.

Being a practical man he decided to sell up. 'I went into early retirement,' he joked, 'so I could enjoy life a bit more. I'm lucky to have enough to live fairly comfortably doing the things I enjoy.' Arthur hasn't retired altogether from the tailoring profession – he is far too active a person for that. He is still very much part of the tailoring brotherhood, but now helps others with his advice born of experience.

Arthur has always been a family man. His home was a really happy, joyful place in which I spent many hours. He shared the hard times in the beginning, when he was building up his business, with Lottie, his wife. And then, just at a time when they might have expected to enjoy a more comfortable lifestyle together, Lottie died tragically of cancer. It shook Arthur for quite a while, but he is the kind of person who never looks back on the past with remorse. 'We were happy as we were', Arthur told me, 'because that is how life treated us at the time. We couldn't have been happier, because money doesn't make happiness. We didn't go on holidays abroad but we enjoyed our weeks at Scarborough or wherever we went. That was our life and we loved it.'

Today Arthur has remarried, and his wife Nancy is just like him. She has seen tragedy, buried a loving husband, had her ups and downs, but like Arthur she lives one day at a time. I believe God has brought them together so that the autumn of their life may be fruitful and happy.

So the simple message of Arthur is to live one

day at a time. Don't look back to the past with remorse or nostalgia and don't be afraid of tomorrow. Live the present moment to the full, and in it you will find all the happiness you need. Jesus said in Matthew, chapter 6, 'Can any of you for all his worrying add one single day to his span of life?' So do not worry about tomorrow. Tomorrow will take care of itself.'

Lord Jesus you are closer to me than my own breathing, as present and as life-giving as my own heart. May each breath I take, and each heart-beat I experience this day deepen my awareness of your presence. I thank you for waking me to the light of day. Grant that I may pass this day in gladness and peace with all those with whom I work and all those whom I meet, so that at day's end I shall know you have been with me because you have been gracious enough to fill my life with your presence.

The Disturbing Gospel

The rich soil is the people with a noble and generous heart who have heard the word and take it to themselves and yield a harvest through their perseverance. (Luke 8: 15)

Many people look on the Bible as a comforting book – a book at bedtime to help them sleep soundly. Its effect on me is often just the opposite. It challenges my life, and I find it most disturbing.

Let me give you an example of what I mean. For years I had campaigned for peace and reconciliation in Northern Ireland. So when the Peace Women started their movement in Northern Ireland in 1976, I convened the first meeting of all those on the mainland who were willing to help them. The meeting was held at the conference centre in Yorkshire, of which I was in charge. Everyone said that the conference was a great success. The finale on Sunday was a Mass.

During the sign of peace, at Mass, instead of the usual greeting 'Peace be with you', I saluted the Peace Women with the words, 'May the Peace of Christ thoroughly disturb you.' I was, of course, speaking to them about their search for peace in their troubled land, but God took my words and turned them back on me. He wanted my peace too. So he disturbed me, and not them.

This is what happened. The Peace People of Northern Ireland were hoping to find inner peace among the bombs and bullets of their towns and cities. But I was too secure in my centre tucked away in a lovely Yorkshire valley to talk to them in a meaningful way about peace. Through a series of events over which I had no control, I was replaced at the conference centre. Then, because of my desire for peace, I was catapulted into Northern Ireland to share the pain of the Peace People. It was the price I had to pay for daring to take the full gospel message into my own life. To try to live up to what I had preached to others; to really believe that God wanted me to work for peace, and have my lifestyle disturbed.

So when I hear Jesus say 'Blessed are the peace makers', I wonder whether we Christians are really honest when we say, 'I am all for peace'. What we often mean, of course, is peace and quiet. The boat of our comfortable lives is not to be rocked. We like to talk about peace rather than live it. It makes us 'feel' good. But now I know that the gospel that is not lived through personal experience is meaningless. It is a string of words which do not compel assent and involvement. Working for peace is a very disturbing way of life.

Through that single personal experience I have discovered that the gospel of Jesus is disturbing, if you take it seriously. In it there are many words like 'forgiveness', 'simplicity', 'suffering', 'healing', 'love', which are essential to the gospel of Jesus Christ. If, as with peace, we try to live out the full meaning of these words, then we will soon find that they will turn our lives upside down. Then these words, like the gospel itself, will disturb us.

Lord, who can grasp all the wealth of one of your words in the gospel? For your words have many shades of meaning. You have coloured your words with many hues, so that each person who studies them can see in them what he loves and what challenges him to live a fuller human, Christian life.

Inner Peace

Peace I bequeath to you, my own peace I give you, a peace that the world cannot give, this is my gift to you. Do not let your hearts be troubled or afraid. (John 14: 27)

Inner peace of mind, heart and soul is what we all seek and desperately need. We may be surprised when we look inside ourselves and see how fragile our own peace is, and how easily it is shattered. We know only too well that peace is as elusive as a butterfly. You snatch at it and, just when you think you have it in the palm of your hand, it is gone. But if you lie still, then it will come in all its beautiful colours and maybe rest on your shoulder. Joe is someone who is blessed with this deep inner, restful peace, but it was not always so.

When I first met him he was anything but peaceful. A sensitive caring person, he was constantly being hurt by people who persistently disturbed any peace he had. Whenever he indulged in feelings of resentment against them he felt very guilty about it, and this upset his relationship with God. His worst failing was his very low appreciation of himself as a person. He felt that inner peace was not for him, and that he only got what he deserved. Joe has been many times to our healing services, and God has used these to help him discover, and appreciate, the true meaning of inner peace – with which he is now blessed. He knows it is a gift that has to be treasured and nourished.

Joe's path to peace began when he started to appreciate himself as a person, warts and all. He saw his value not only in God's eyes but in his own as well. Gradually the exaggerated feelings of guilt, fear, tension, and the thousand and one other things which disturbed him, ceased to dominate his life. He became more at peace within himself, more secure. And the people who had earlier disturbed his peace now now longer played on his mind. They no longer caused him to lose his deep inner peace.

'Before I came to the healing services,' he told me, 'there were people in my life to whom I was like a red rag to a bull and they to me. Whenever we met, however good my intentions were, I always left their company deeply disturbed in my spirit. We were oil and water to each other. It seemed they couldn't help what they were doing, and I just couldn't overcome my spontaneous negative reaction to them. I thought of what Jesus said about turning the other cheek. I tried to do this time and time again, but the result was always the same. Then I realized that my contacts with them were destroying me as a person, and that surely God didn't want that. So I started not so much to avoid them deliberately, as not to seek their company. Gradually my inner spirit and memories were healed, and I began to pray for those who hurt me and to really wish them well in their lives. Whenever we meet I commit the encounter to God my father, and he sees me through. It's strange, but the aggro and hassle seem to have disappeared. In some cases we have been able to talk deeply and reasonably to each other and become friends. But still there are many with whom I have not reached this state of peace and who would disturb me if I stayed for a long time in their company. I know myself and my limitations. I never cross the frontiers, but thank God that the frontiers are being pushed further back and are not manned by hostile forces.'

Joe has, I think found the secret of inner peace. Turning the other cheek is, for him, wishing everyone well and not engaging in negative conflict. Like Jesus he has forgiven from his heart all those who have hurt him. But he is aware how fragile his inner peace is. That is why he protects it and will not stretch it beyond its limits. He knows that the peace of soul, which he now has, is God's special gift to him. He values it when, like a butterfly, it comes and rests on his shoulder.

Lord Jesus, giver of inner peace, I pray that you will turn my heart to you this day in the depths of my being where with the noise of the world round me stilled and my mind at rest I may find you present to me as the giver and sharer of my peace.

Heroines

Jesus took Peter and James with him. And a sudden fear came over him, and great distress. And he said to them, 'My soul is sorrowful to the point of death. Wait here, and keep awake.' (Mark 14: 33–4)

We all have problems which worry us. Problems which we know we need to share with those nearest and dearest to us. Jesus had problems the night before he died, and so he took three of his closest friends with him into a quiet garden where they could spend an hour together. He needed to share his problems with them. If we have a problem which worries us because we don't know how to break it to our loved ones, perhaps the story of Joan will help us.

Joan never had things easy in her life. She had to bring up seven children more or less on her own. When they were all reared and she could reasonably have expected a more relaxed lifestyle, it was then that tragedy struck a cruel blow. A few years ago she discovered a lump in her breast, and was shattered when her doctor diagnosed cancer. She was very optimistic that it would not be too serious, but yet a nagging doubt remained at the back of her mind that it might be worse than she imagined. Sensitively she shared her worry with her children. She didn't want to make them anxious, and so her attitude to them was 'I'll be all right'. They encouraged her to undergo the usual rather severe medical treatment. She made an excellent recovery after what was considered to be a very successful operation.

Then the really big problem arose. Last year secondaries of cancer appeared, and the prognosis this time was poor. She was very honest in talking to me about it. 'This was a great challenge to my faith. For weeks everything was a desert round me. It was only gradually through prayer and thinking things out with God that I came to terms with my condition. From then on I received a deep inner peace which is the most wonderful thing in my life. And it was because of this peace that I could share deeply with my children.'

She undertook something which I consider was remarkably brave. Strengthened by her inner peace, she went individually to the homes of each of her children and told them of her condition. She did it in a way unique to each one of them, and she managed to convey her peace to them. She broke the news in a way which each one could understand and accept. Some took it much harder than others because, I suppose, that's the way they are made.

Last summer she arranged for all the family to have a holiday together. It was a holiday they will always remember as the one in which they grew closer together, as a family, than ever before. One of her daughters said it was 'indescribable. We were all so incredibly happy that it seemed to change our whole outlook on life.'

At Christmas I went to visit Joan. She was radiant – there is no other word to describe how she looked. Her flat was full of flowers and gaily coloured cards, and a beautiful Christmas tree. She was surrounded by her children and grandchildren. A few weeks later she died peacefully as her seven children held hands round her bed. They had shared a problem together. They were able to see death not as the end of everything. 'Mummy shared everything with us,' said her eldest daughter, 'and now we know she is at peace. She shares that peace with us too.'

Lord Jesus, you shared your moments of great joy and deep sorrow with those who were your closest friends; teach us the value of sharing. Teach us that we were not meant to live and die alone but as members of the human family, and that in sharing with others we are really sharing with you.

Happiness

I have told you this so that my own joy may be in you and your joy be complete. (John 15: 11)

Whenever anyone asks me if I'm happy I always reply, 'I'd be worried if I wasn't.' Life is meant to be happy. It is very precious and I want to live it to the full. I know I'll never do that unless I'm happy. For me happiness is being glad I'm me and that I have a purpose in my life which God has given to me. If I don't, or can't, love myself then I will never be able to love anyone else. I know that to be happy means I have to share my life, my hopes, my dreams with other people. I'm happy when I share a few thoughts with you, because this is exactly what I want to be doing.

I can't be happy only on the outside. I have to be happy on the inside too – or else I am just presenting a false smile to the world. So for me happiness is really peace of mind. I know that I have a purpose in life, and I *hope* that in some way I am just carrying that out. I can't be certain that I always follow my goal, but then the challenge of trying to reach out towards my destiny is what makes life exciting. God

protect us from secure people who lead a very shel-
tered, closed-in life! They never venture out from
their nest, never fly – but they often envy others
who do.

Life is an adventure, a search for faith. A prayer
which expresses this searching was written some
years ago by an American monk, Thomas Merton:

Lord, I do not see the road ahead of me. I cannot
know for certain where it will end. Nor do I really
know myself. The fact that I think I am following
your will does not mean that I am actually doing
so. But I believe that the desire to please you does
in fact please you. And I hope I have that desire
in all that I am doing.

But how do you find love and happiness? Money,
sang the Beatles, can't buy me love. It can't buy us
happiness either. Jesus knew that. He said that we
were to enjoy life and that life was more important
than jewels, fine clothes or anything else. Jesus
enjoyed life. Do you remember his first miracle at
Cana in Galilee? It was at a wedding feast when the
wine ran out and the party was threatened with
premature closure! Jesus told the head waiter to fill
six stone jars with water. Each jar could hold twenty
or thirty gallons, and the servants, St John wrote,
'filled them to the brim'. No half measures here!
Then they poured the contents out for the guests,
and it was wine of the highest order. Jesus used his
special powers to provide the guests with between
960 and 1440 pints of very special wine. I'm not
saying that drinking a lot of wine makes you happy,

but I am stressing the fact that Jesus wanted the young couple and their guests to remember that wedding day as something very special.

Anyone who reads the gospel with an open mind and heart will know that Jesus loved life, and he told his followers that he had come so that they might have life and have it to the full. St Paul, in his letters to the early Church, stressed this time and again. 'What I want is your happiness,' he said, 'Again, I repeat, what I want is your happiness.' Remember Pope John XXIII, the small, well-rounded pope who was called good Pope John'? He said that you couldn't be a Christian and be a prophet of doom and gloom.

But it isn't easy to be always full of life and happiness, especially when we are surrounded by the terrible violence and selfishness of our world. Somehow we have to try to rise above them, to look at the bright side of life. Satchmo Armstrong, one of my favourite musicians, always touched me when he sang 'It's a beautiful world'. You and I have a right and a duty to be happy. We need each other. So let's start by lighting ourselves up from inside with peace and joy for the good things in our life. They are many, if only we take time to count our blessings. Then together we can look out on a brave new world in which we are glad to share, to be fully alive, to be happy.

Lord Jesus, let me live this day to the full. Let me fill it with all the wonder and joy I knew when I was a child. Let me trust and welcome with an open mind and heart all those whom I encounter today, so that at evening time I may feel that in some way I have contributed to the joy and peace of the world which you entered so humbly and hopefully that we might have life to the full.

Christian Joy

Jesus said, 'You must love the Lord your God with all your heart, with all your soul, with all your mind and with all your strength. You must love your neighbour as yourself. There is no commandment greater than these.' (Mark 12: 30–1)

Going to church should be a source of great joy and happiness. Yet so many people look upon church-going as a bore and a chore, as something that has to be done. When seen entering or leaving a church they often do not look happy or have a smile on their faces. John is a typical example of those church-going people who are high on religion and low on faith.

John came to church in my parish religiously every Sunday. He made sure his wife and children did too. For him it was a duty to be done. That was the way his parents had brought him up, and that was the way he intended to bring up his family. Yet it was obvious that he was not experiencing the full freedom and joy of being a Christian. He was 'tight' within himself. There was no give, no joy in him.

I don't think he appreciated my understanding of

God. You see, all my life I have always preached that God loves us as our Father – that he wants us to be happy, to be free to fly like eagles, and not be like little birds trapped in a cage. This emphasis on joy and freedom worried John, because for him the important thing in religion was the letter of the law. He rejected any idea which threatened the established way of looking at religion. So I decided to have a quiet word with him so that we could come to understand each other a little better. It was one of the most difficult conversations I have had with anyone in my life, because he was so self-righteous, so convinced he was right about everything.

What really, really bugged him was my emphasis on God as a loving father. 'I never had a loving father as a child,' he told me coldly. 'My father saw any sign of affection as weakness. He was a good, law-abiding man, but he was strict. He took no excuses. That's how I imagine God to be. And so I respect God, even fear him, but I don't love him.' I felt sad that John's experience of his own father made it so difficult for him to know the fatherly love of God. No matter how I tried I could not break through the barrier that John erected between himself and anyone who preached the love of God. In his eyes I was diluting his belief that heaven had to be earned the hard way, and that going to church was a duty rather than something to be enjoyed.

John and I have talked and tried to pray together many times, but his healing is still a long way off. And it seems such a shame because he is a good man, though not a happy one. I have shared with his children so that now they realize to some extent that God loves them, and that the Christian life is meant to be full and peaceful. But I'm afraid they have been damaged by their father's mistaken approach to God. One day perhaps, they will help him to realize the real purpose of going to church, and to understand the joy and happiness of being human and being a Christian.

Faith is, I believe, God's gift to us, and religion is the way we express it in our culture, rules, outlook and general behaviour. The Christian faith is, for example, one of love, joy and hope, and proclaims the unity of everyone in Christ. It is a source of peace not only for the individual but for nations. Christian religion unfortunately falls far short of this ideal. It is often the cause of division, dissension and war. History underlines this sad fact. Faith is expressed in love while religious exercises are often expressed out of a sense of duty.

Jesus came on earth to heal us and make us whole persons. 'I have come', he said, 'that you might have life, and have it to the full.' He wants his joy to be ours as well. If we are a happy people then going to church will be what it was meant to be. A time for celebration. A time for sharing with others our times of sadness, our times of true joy and happiness, because we know God is our loving Father. And surely that should make us happy and joyful.

Lord Jesus, you came among us to show by your example that love is the greatest commandment without which all religious observances are meaningless. Fill our hearts with love for God our Father whose children we are, and through love may we live at peace with our neighbour and within ourselves.

The Good Samaritan

A Samaritan traveller was moved with compassion when he saw him. He went up and bandaged his wounds, pouring oil and wine on them. He then lifted him up on his own mount, carried him to the inn and looked after him. Next day, he took out two denarii and handed them to the inn-keeper. 'Look after him,' he said, 'and on my way back I will make good any extra expense you have.' (Luke 10: 33–5)

I never cease to be amazed that on many occasions when I needed help, it came from a most unexpected source. I have come across many good samaritans in my lifetime. The most unlikely people seemed to turn up from nowhere and get me out of a tight corner. I would like to tell you about a good samaritan who helped me a few months ago.

I had invited a young couple who were close friends to celebrate their engagement. It was to be an occasion to remember, and so I chose a very special meal at my favourite restaurant set in the heart of the Yorkshire Dales, about twenty miles from my home. The evening went like a dream, and it was filled with the laughter of true happiness.

We didn't want it to end. We were driving home afterwards feeling on top of the world and saying what a perfect evening it was, when *it* happened. A red light started flashing on the dashboard of my car, and we were reduced to silence by fear of the impending doom. It came even sooner than we expected. The engine cut out completely, and we slowly moved to a halt.

What a let down! We pretended it was something very temporary at first, and more in hope than anticipation I made many fruitless attempts to get the engine started. Eventually this only served to increase our frustration. The evening air was cold, and my friends began to feel uncomfortable. We decided that we had run out of petrol, and so the best thing to do was to get a passing motorist to stop and take us to the nearest petrol station six miles away. We signalled several drivers in their sleek cars, but they ignored our frantic pleas for help.

I had just decided to walk to the petrol station when down the road, its radio blaring pop music, came a car which seemed to be falling apart at the seams. As it shot past us we made no attempt to stop it. But about fifty yards up the road it screeched to a halt and reversed quickly towards us. Out of the car, still blaring its strident music, stepped the driver. A typical hippie with shoulder-length hair, ear-rings, gaudy rings on all his fingers, and a leather jacket festooned with badges. 'Need any help?' he asked. I mumbled something above the music about running out of petrol. Before I could say another word he was back in his car roaring up the hill. That was the last I thought we would see of him.

But I was wrong. Fifteen minutes later he was back again with a gallon of precious petrol. He poured it into the car as I haltingly thanked him for his kindness. In fact I was really apologizing for my rash judgement of him. 'We'll be all right now,' I said. 'Try it to make sure,' he told me, 'just in case it might be something else.' I turned the ignition. The engine remained dead. The young man said, 'I know a bit about cars. Let me have a go.' And there he was inside the bonnet with his torch, testing the hundred and one mysterious things that could have gone wrong. And then he lay under the car with little care for his clothes until finally, after an hour, he got the car going. I stood by amazed, not knowing what to say and yet wanting to thank him profusely for all he had done.

When I tried to pay him for his services, all he would accept was the price of the gallon of petrol. 'That's enough,' he said, 'you'd do the same for me if I was stranded.' Then he was off into the night, the car music louder than ever. I thought of the man in the Bible helped by the Good Samaritan, and of those who passed by on the other side who should have helped. That young man made the Bible story come alive for me. He saved our evening and left us with its most precious memory: the hippie who helped us when we were stranded on a lonely country road.

Lord Jesus, who was wounded for our sins that we might be healed, and live the new life of grace, we thank you for all those who throughout our lives have come unbidden to our aid. They have been the Good Samaritans who have made the gospel come alive for us. Grant that we too may always consider it a privilege to come to the assistance of the stranger, knowing that whenever we assist him we are really tending the wounded Christ in him.

Brief Encounter

When Jesus saw Nathaniel coming towards him he said of him, 'Here is a man who deserves the name Nathaniel, meaning incapable of deceit.' 'How do you know me?' said Nathaniel. 'Before Philip came to call you', said Jesus, 'I saw you under the fig tree.' (John 1: 47–8)

Life is very strange. We sometimes meet people in a brief encounter, and later are amazed at the significance it has in our lives. One of the most dramatic encounters I had was in Belfast a few years ago. Let me first give you the background to that meeting so that you may appreciate how extraordinary it was for me.

In the early 'sixties Tom Burke, a young Irishman from Cork, came to Leeds looking for work. Partly, I suppose, because I was from his native city, he felt very much at ease in my company, and we soon became friends. A likeable hard-working and open-hearted young man, he was very popular, and as with so many of us he came to look on England as his home. At his request, whenever I visited Cork, I called on his parents to give them up-to-date news

81

on their son, and to reassure them that all was well with him.

After a few years Tom met and married a lovely Yorkshire lass. Their wedding was a very happy occasion and one which I shall always remember. They had two sons and a daughter whom I had the privilege of christening.

Time moved on twenty years. By then I was heavily involved in working for peace in Northern Ireland. During one of my visits to Belfast, I decided one evening to walk through the streets of one of the troubled areas and experience for myself what it was like to live there. It was raining heavily, and so after a while I took shelter in the corner of a street. I noticed an army patrol coming down the road, running then crouching, guns poised at the ready as they covered each other in this dangerously hostile area.

A soldier came running along the pavement and took up a crouching position next to me. Even though his face was blackened I was aware of the tension in his body. I knew he was conscious of my presence standing behind him in the shadows. At first he said nothing. Then suddenly, without turning his head, he spoke to me quietly. 'Aren't you Monsignor Buckley? You baptized me, Father. I'm Tom Burke's son.' I couldn't believe my ears. 'What are you doing here?' he asked. I mumbled something about working for peace, and that God wanted me here. 'I suppose he wants me here too,' he said. 'Pray for me, Father, and please tell my Dad I'm all right.' Then he was gone, running down the street into the darkness and the rain. I stood there too shocked to move.

I never thought when I first met Tom Burke, the shy-eyed Irishman, that one day I would meet his son in a soldier's uniform in such a violent situation. I prayed in my heart for Tom and his son; that nothing would happen to him that night, or any night, that would hurt his father. I prayed for peace that we could all live and even laugh together on the streets of Belfast. As I continued my journey up the road, the wetness on my cheeks was not caused by the rain.

That brief encounter made me realize that none of us can foresee the future. Who can tell where we will be or what we will be doing ten years from now? We have to trust the future, as we do the present, to God the Father's loving care. But wherever we are, or however difficult the situation may be, may we look on all whom we meet with love and peace. It was a brief encounter that rainy night in Belfast between the soldier and the priest. It was a meeting which made me pray for peace in our world and, please God, in our time.

Lord Jesus, you know that even though the future is hidden from our eyes, our attitude today can influence what is yet to come in our lives. Help us so to live in peace that future generations will find no cause in us for the widening of divisions or the fostering of violence but may we live in harmony and peace with everyone, and by our words and actions may we be true peacemakers so that we can be called children of God our Father.

Healing

That evening, after sunset, they brought to him all who were sick and those who were possessed by devils. The whole town came crowding round the door, and he cured many who were suffering from diseases of one kind or another. (Mark 1: 32–4)

I believe in healing. I have a very good personal reason for doing so. When I was just five years old, I came home from a school friend's birthday party and proceeded to get violently sick. After about an hour my mother became very anxious and sent for the family doctor. By the time he arrived I was beginning to lose consciousness, and so he had me whisked off to hospital. That night I lapsed into a coma. Two other doctors were summoned, and they diagnosed an acute form of food poisoning. They said that there was nothing they or anybody else could do for me. All that was to be done now was to wait for the end.

I was fed intravenously. Medicine not being so advanced then as it is today I still carry the marks on my body where the tubes were inserted in my chest and thighs. I lay there in a comatose state for six days, and I am told that my face was a deathly purple. Subconsciously I heard the comings and goings of my family, and the quiet sobbing of my mother who never seemed to leave the bedside. It was an eerie feeling as if I was watching it all. I can still remember it today as vividly as if it was yesterday.

Then the healing happened. On the sixth day after my admission to hospital, the matron, Sister Raymond, a nun, wrapped me in a blanket and brought me and my parents to the convent chapel, 'Come on,' I am told she said, 'Let's see what God can do.' She laid me on the altar and offered my life to the Lord. She spoke to God in a very personal way in her own words as if he were her closest friend. I still hear her voice, but how I did I shall never know, because I was unconscious. Later that morning I remember opening my eyes and holding my hands out to my mother, and asking for a drink. Within three days I was back home again much to the great joy of my parents.

Years later, as a priest, I returned to see a much older Sister Raymond, now retired, to ask her how and why she did it. Had she special powers? Her answer was simple and direct. 'I felt for your parents, especially your mother. I thought it such a shame to see such a young child dying from such a simple thing as eating something wrong at a birthday, so I just asked God to heal you and he did.' She had never read a book on healing, never laid hands for healing on anyone and yet she was the one who was the minister of my healing. 'Did you ever heal anyone else?' I asked. 'Whenever I believe that someone should live,' she said, 'then I ask God to heal them. After all he is their Father and he should care about them.'

A very simple story. A true one. I know because it concerns me. That is why I believe that when we are ill, or someone we love is sick, then we should pray for healing. The very asking for it is a healing process. Our prayers may not be answered the way we want, but they will be answered. In that particular way we will be healed.

Lord Jesus Christ, you came on earth to heal a broken-hearted and wounded world. You had compassion on those who called on you for help and healing. You touched the sick and guilt-laden, and they walked away in health and freedom of spirit. Come this day to all who call on your holy name, and visit them with your saving power, so that they too may be released in mind and body to praise and thank you for your love and compassion.

Encouragement

Bless our God and make his praise resound, who brings our soul to live and keeps our feet from faltering. (Psalm 66: 8–9)

We all need encouragement. It lifts us up and brings out the best in us. We all need people who will encourage us to develop our talents, who are glad when we succeed. They have our welfare at heart, and really want us to do well and be happy. How often have we been tempted to give up or go for the soft option when the going gets tough, but then we meet people who have confidence in us. Their support is the deciding factor which turns what might have been failure into success.

So we think of, and are grateful for, friends who have helped us along the road of life and have encouraged us to become the type of people we are. They would be amazed if we were to tell them of the goodness that passed from their life into ours. What an influence for good they have had on us by just being there, and by our knowing that they are our friends! They were the rock on which we stood firm when we could so easily have been plunged into gloom and despair.

In my work I meet so many people broken by negative criticism. Psychiatrists and community workers say that the majority of people live at only a tenth of their potential. Much that is good and creative in their lives never sees the light of day. Why? Because they have not been encouraged to grow as individuals and develop their own particular talents. They have been crushed by circumstances, and by people around them who tell them they will never change things, and so they feel beaten even before they start. What would have happened, for example, to Christy Brown if he had not been encouraged by his mother to write and paint. Christy was physically crippled from birth and never went to school. Unable to use his hands he wrote and painted with his feet. In that broken body there was a hidden genius which came out under the warmth of love and encouragement.

It is our privilege as human beings and Christians to help people to grow as full human beings. They may be crippled in mind rather than body, but we will continue to be amazed at the transformation they undergo when we encourage them. When I first met Mother Teresa of Calcutta shortly after she began her work for the dying and homeless in Calcutta, she told me that the help and encouragement she received from sympathetic people made all the difference to the growth and scope of her ministry of mercy. True, she is gifted with a profound and compassionate faith, but God too needs help from us if we want his specially gifted people to spread their wings and fly.

Martin is a young man blind from the age of three. He has climbed Snowdonia and done all sorts of exciting things which we as sighted people would never dream of doing, because we think they are beyond us. Martin says, 'Life is thrilling. It is full of challenges, and whether I succeed or not at least I've tried. I'm not going to sit in a corner and let life pass me by. I'm still young, and my blindness has taught me that the fact I can't see is not the end of everything. The opposite is true. Through the encouragement of others, my blindness has spurred me on and helped me to grow as a person and to enjoy life.'

The Christian faith is all about encouragement – lifting people up, so that they are filled with hope and not despair. Jesus was the great encourager. That is why the lepers, the poor, the no-hopers flocked to hear him talk about the meaning of life and how God the Father loves us all individually as his children. Jesus said life was more than food and clothes. It is that something deep inside us that makes us aware that life is worth living, that it has a purpose, and that we are somebody. If we don't love ourselves, then how can we be happy and love anyone else? The person who is fulfilled encourages others to find fulfilment. The kind word we speak today, or the genuine smile we give others, may be all they need to lift them up. Don't forget, this is our world, and if we encourage each other we will be happy together, and life really will be worth living.

Lord Jesus, almighty Son of God, you too needed encouragement during your ministry on earth. We praise you that in your risen life you are our great encourager, because even when we walk in the valley of darkness you are there as the good shepherd with your crook and staff to give us comfort. Help us today in word and deed to be a source of encouragement to all those whom we meet.

Contentment

In the morning, long before dawn, Jesus got up and left the house, and went off to a lonely place and prayed there. (Mark 1: 35)

I have often said to myself in the middle of a busy day, 'Oh how I wish I had time to myself for some peace and quiet.' But I wasn't really being honest with myself. You see, we all have the time if we use it properly. And if it seems we haven't, then we have to make time.

Jesus did. He was aware of the strains and stresses made on him by the demands of the people round about him. He slipped off on his own to quiet places like the desert or mountains, or to the peace of a garden, so that he could think about his life and what he was doing with it. He needed to be at peace with himself and his world. He knew contentment, a contentment we all need.

Let me tell you a story of what I mean by contentment. Last summer I went to the Pyrenees for my holidays. One day I went for a walk up a wooded hillside. After a few miles the path gave way to an open stretch of meadow with a stream flowing swiftly through it. The sun glinting through the trees made the water sparkle like diamonds. I sat down to rest, and soon all the tiredness of my body and spirit seemed to melt away. I noticed an elderly couple further down the bank. They blended into the scene perfectly, and must have been there many times before. I watched them. They were in harmony with one another. Her hands were busy with her knitting needles, while he was having fun with his dog who fetched the sticks he threw into the stream. They were obviously happy. They had found time for peace and quiet in which to relax. Here, I thought, is what life is all about.

I continued my journey, and at a bend in the stream I saw a very tall man fishing. He blended so well with the scenery that he was barely discernible from the grass and the trees surrounding him. I watched him in silence, careful not to disturb him. Gently he moved his fishing line across the water, much as an artist strokes his brush on the canvas. I knew that he was aware of my presence though he showed no sign of it. He was at peace, and he was doing something which gave him a sense of fulfilment. He moved gently upstream, but before leaving he turned round and gave a friendly nod in my direction. I think we both appreciated each other's presence, and the value of silence.

Today more and more people in our noisy world are searching for something which will bring them peace of mind and soul. What John Donne says is true, 'No man is an island.' But each of us has to find an island within ourselves where noise is stilled and we can begin to experience the soothing, healing power of peace. We may not be able to go to a peaceful river scene, but we need to allow peace to enter our minds and hearts. Contentment is not so much a place as an attitude of mind.

Just as in human relationships there are times spent talking together about every conceivable subject under the sun, so there are times – if I want to know myself and others better – that I have to be silent. I know speech is the normal form of communication, but there is a whole new world of self-discovery which I can only undertake in reflective silence. Silence challenges me with its truth, and if I want inner peace then I have to listen to its message. Through it I can enter into the pain of others, and hear the tears which they weep deep inside themselves. This form of silence is the best form of communication in any attempts we make to minister in healing to others and to ourselves.

In silence we will grow in peace within ourselves and with each other. 'Be still and know I am with you,' says God. He wants to share his peace with us. But like the three people I met in the Pyrenees, we need to be quiet sometimes if we want to experience what the peace of contentment really means.

Lord Jesus Christ, great communicator with people and lover of silence, help me to reflect on you deep within myself, so that with the noise of the busy world stilled I may in silence find you, and in finding you discover my true self.

Alcoholism

I fail to carry out the things I want to do, and I find myself doing the very things I hate. Though the will to do what is good is in me, the performance is not. Who will rescue me? Thanks be to God through Jesus Christ our Lord. (Romans 7: 15, 18, 24–25)

They say, Once an alcoholic, always an alcoholic. Very little hope of being any different is ever held out to them. But James is different. He *was* an alcoholic in the sense that he could not control his use of alcohol; it controlled him. He isn't today. Let me tell you the story how this came about. Twenty-one years ago he married Celia. They were very much in love. A year after their marriage James started drinking. This became progressively worse, until Celia had no option but to separate from him for the sake of the children. She loved him, but although they made several attempts to get together again, James' drinking always came in between. It hurt him deeply. He knew he was hurting himself as well as Celia and the family but, despite all his good intentions, once he met up with his mates he was very soon down the slippery slope of drinking too much.

Two years ago he came to a few of our healing sessions and it seemed he was healed. We were all so happy, especially Celia. All went well for six months and then at Christmas he 'broke out'. Hopes were dashed, tears were shed and once more James had left home. Celia thought this was the end of the road, because now it seemed as if God couldn't help him.

He returned to Ireland and every day Celia prayed that a miracle would happen, and that James would be able to overcome his drinking habits. His mother, to whom James was very attached, prayed for this also. It was a long, lonely and testing time. Suddenly, things changed dramatically. James' mother died. This shook James to the roots of his spirit, and as if by some extraordinary revelation he realized overnight all the pain he had caused his mother, Celia, his children and those whom he loved.

He returned to Celia and they both knew in a way which they could not put into words that James was now different. At first his daughters refused to accept him, because they had never known him except as an alcoholic. James and Celia took it patiently. Eventually, the girls could see for themselves that James was different. Today he is everything a husband and father should be. His Catholic faith means a great deal to him. Whenever he gets depressed he is aware of his mother's presence and how long and well she prayed for him. With this memory before him the clouds soon pass away. Of course he has the odd bout of drinking and I suppose you would say that therefore he is not fully healed, but these bouts are certainly less frequent and less severe. Most of all he knows he now has the power within himself which will conquer the 'demon drink'. He is becoming more and more in control of himself because he knows, as I have told him time and time again, he must live one day at a time, and be aware of the weakness within himself. He believes that God is with him but also that he needs to help himself. Healing is not left to God alone. We share in the healing process with him.

Now I don't claim to understand James's case completely, no more than I can grasp the vice-like grip which drink has over some people. I know that most people who are plagued by alcoholism live the miracle of not drinking just one day at a time. They are beautiful people, and I admire them tremendously. They have learned to turn their addiction into something very positive and creative. But we can pray and hope that all who struggle against alcohol can change. With God all things are possible. They certainly are with James. His desire to control his drinking habits turned his face to God. I believe he will never be beaten if he keeps his eyes in that direction.

Father, there are times in our lives when we are so oppressed by difficulties on all sides, and so aware of our own feelings, that we are inclined to surrender. At times like these may we be lifted up in the strong arms of your

Son and through him find the courage to continue our struggle, knowing that in your name the victory will eventually be ours.

The Peace Nun

Though I live surrounded by trouble you keep me alive. You stretch your hand out and save me, your love is everlasting.
(Psalm 138: 7–8)

Good news out of Belfast is as rare as orchids growing in the desert. But Sister Genevieve is good news. If ever there was a peacemaker in that troubled and divided city then she is one. She has raised, through St Louise's College, of which she was for many years head mistress, a whole generation of young women whose outlook is new, creative and peaceful. St Louise's College is a remarkable school and Sister Genevieve a remarkable person. Let me tell you about her and her girls whom she has helped to form into people of vision and peace.

Sister Genevieve, born in Dublin, entered the Sisters of Charity to dedicate her life to helping the less fortunate in the world. Sent to Belfast to teach, she was soon appointed head of St Louise's College, one of the largest Catholic schools in Europe. She is an inspiring and determined leader, who wants what is best for those under her care. The girls come mainly from troubled areas of the city, and many of them have known tragedy in their families. Sister Genevieve has taught them that out of the ashes of the present they must build the future. If they are to look back on the past, it is only to learn from its mistakes. The future lies in their hands.

Genevieve encourages and inspires her 'family', teachers and students, to have a pride in themselves. Each one is helped to become aware of her own individuality and value. Sister Genevieve is slow to accept excuses for second best, and so every morning the girls come up the Falls Road to St Louise's in spotless uniforms; they are well turned-out, even if some of them come from deprived homes. They pass scenes of yet another incident of the previous night, with burned-out cars, but they are on their way to school. Tomorrow, when their turn comes they will help to build a brave and better new world. Sister Genevieve says so, and they know it.

Her idea of education is very wide. The choice is so varied in her school that St Louise's College has been awarded a special prize for excellence in school curriculum and innovation in teaching. She wants her girls to have a rounded education, to travel abroad and widen their experience of life. She has also made them aware of what other Christians believe and practise. Her school welcomes ministers and leaders who are of other Churches and faiths to explain what they believe. There are debating and dramatic societies, and sporting events with boys and girls of Methodist and state schools. It is hoped that through these they will learn from experience that they have nothing to fear from each other.

Genevieve has now retired from the headship and is busier than ever with groups throughout Belfast and farther afield. She is spreading her message of a new world of peace for the young. Jesus said, 'Blessed are the peacemakers, they shall be called children of God'. True, there may not be orchids in the desert, but Sister Genevieve and her girls bring us good news from Belfast.

Lord Jesus Christ, grant that in whatever dangers we are placed we may always call upon your name because you are the shepherd and you will lead us into fresh pastures, where peace will reign and the terror of darkness will be no more.

Silent Night

Today in the town of David a saviour has been born to you; he is Christ the Lord. And here is a sign for you; you will find a baby wrapped in swaddling clothes and lying in a manger. And suddenly with the angel there was a throng of the heavenly host, praising God and singing: Glory to God in the highest heaven, and peace to men who enjoy his favour. (Luke 2: 11–14)

We all love to sing carols at Christmas time and the most popular is 'Silent Night'. I have sung it over the years in widely different circumstances, but the most poignant time for me was when I heard it sung, nearly forty-five years ago, in a refugee camp on the outskirts of Rome. These refugee camps were scattered all over Europe for dispossessed persons who had no relatives, no passports, no identity, no nation which wanted them within its boundaries. They were nameless, faceless people, many of whom had been the victims of concentration camps.

The refugee camp in Rome housed several thousand people who were forced to live in the most appalling sub-human conditions. Even though it was Christmas time there seemed little cause for hope, or any reason for them to celebrate Christmas. As students, some of us were asked to help with a Mass which was to be said in the camp. It was the first time I had been to such a place, and the memory chills the heart.

A makeshift altar was set up for the occasion in the dismal and muddy surroundings of what was rather exaggeratedly called the 'exercise yard'. It was a bleak setting. The night was bitterly cold, and the only thing to cheer the pathetic scene was the brightness of the stars in a clear blue winter's sky and the spluttering candles on the makeshift altar. In the dim light I could see people moving out from their huts and huddling together for warmth as Mass began. There was an eerie silence about the whole proceedings which will always stay in my memory. It seemed such a hopeless situation in which to talk about the birth of God's Son who was supposed to bring peace on earth. Then gently, in the corner of the exercise yard, someone rather hesitantly started to sing the first notes of 'Silent Night'.

The notes hung in the evening air, at once an inspiration and a challenge. Gradually the singer was joined by others in the compound until the volume of human voices finding new strength and courage swelled into a huge choir. The air was full of the most beautiful heart-warming sound, as if the angels themselves were joining in the song of praise to the God of peace. It was a carol of joy from a place of despair. Each one sang in his own language the words of the Christmas carol, the carol they knew so well and which reminded them of their homelands and those things of the spirit which they held dear. In the midst of such horrendous suffering they, who had so little, found hope to believe again in a God who loved them and would see them through. Never again will 'Silent Night' sound so sweetly or so meaningfully for those of us who saw Christ come alive in a refugee camp where people who were homeless found a home with all the warmth of its memories.

So, as we think of the humble stable in which God's only son was born let us spare a thought for all those refugees throughout the world who have been driven out of their homes and country by violence. May Christ, the homeless baby who came to share his first Christmas with us, help them find homes again, either in their own country or a new land, and may their homes be once again filled with the peace of which the angels sang.

Father, no one is a stranger to you, and no one is ever far from your loving care. In your kindness watch over refugees and exiles – those separated from their loved ones and those who are homeless – and bring them safely to the place where they long to be. Help us always to show your kindness to them and to see in them the image of your Son, who came on earth to share our home so that one day we might share with him in his heavenly home.

Against the Odds

We are in difficulties on all sides, but never cornered; we see no answer to our problems, but never despair. (2 Corinthians 4: 8)

Too many people bow down under difficulties. They quickly admit defeat, but when we are prepared to fight against the odds, for what we believe to be right, great things happen. This was so in Jesus' life. He had to battle against all sorts of prejudices in order to prove who he was, and what was his purpose in life. My story is of someone who battled against the odds all her life, and who won through because of her courage and Christian conviction.

Mary comes from Cork in Ireland. She was only seventeen when her mother died. She immediately left school to stay at home and look after the family. She longed to marry and have a family of her own, but rarely went to dances or social occasions where she could meet someone whom she might marry. Then when she was just turned forty she met and married Jim. They had a lovely daughter, Betty.

Eighteen months later tragedy struck. Jim died

suddenly of coronary thrombosis. Mary was absolutely devastated. One would have expected her to crumble under the blow. But she was made of sterner stuff. She wanted Betty to have a brother or sister, and so she decided to try to adopt a baby. Three years later she read in a local paper of a deaf and dumb baby girl whom no one wanted to adopt. Mary offered to adopt the baby.

Everything was against her, including her age; she was now 46. She was widowed, and no widow of that age in Ireland had been allowed in recent years to adopt a child. All her family were against the adoption. Even her brother, a priest, used his influence to try to persuade her and the authorities against the move. But Mary won, after a long struggle of four years. She adopted Joan and immediately started to learn speech therapy as well as sign language. When Joan went to a school for the partially hearing, Mary was sufficiently qualified in speech therapy to apply for and secure a post in the same school.

Today, at the age of twenty, Joan can speak and hear in a way that would have seemed impossible years ago. She is respected by others as a normally hearing person. This is a dream come true for Mary and herself.

Over the years meanwhile Mary became a highly qualified speech therapist, and to this work she devoted all her time. Many young men and women who have overcome their speech handicap owe their present position to her painstaking care. They are part of her extended family, all because she had the courage and faith to fight against the odds. Today she has retired, but she continues to work for those with a hearing and speech handicap. It is her way of saying thanks for what has happened to herself and Joan in their lives. Christ has promised us, 'I am with you. Come to me all who are overburdened and I will give you new strength.' When the odds are stacked against us, we are not alone. Christ is there helping us with his presence and his power. With him on our side we will win through.

Lord, show us how to be generous and not to count the cost. By the light of your wisdom, may we follow our conscience and so fulfil your loving plan for our lives. May we find fulfilment especially when we meet the challenges of life with faith, trust and generosity of spirit.

Faith and Fear

It began to blow a gale and the waves were breaking into the boat so that it was almost swamped. But Jesus was in the stern, his head on the cushion, asleep. They woke him and said to him, 'Master, do you not care? We are going down!' And he woke up and he rebuked the wind and said to the sea, 'Quiet now! Be calm!' And the wind dropped, and all was calm again. Then he said to them, 'Why are you so frightened? How is it that you have no faith?' (Mark 4: 37–40)

We have all experienced fear at some time in our lives. It can bring life to a standstill. Let me tell you what happened when fear took a hold of me.

It was about seven years ago when I had some awful pains in my stomach. I ignored them at first, presuming that they could be caused by something I had eaten which disagreed with me. It could be anything. Whenever I was in company, or doing something, the pains seemed to disappear. Was it all imagination? Was the pain something in my mind?

Anyway, as time went on the pains got worse. I couldn't sleep at night. It's pretty awful to twist and turn in your bed, wondering what on earth is wrong inside you. I would get up two or three times during the night to make myself a cup of tea. Then I would sit in my dressing gown reading the previous day's paper to while away the time. It was all very lonely. How I pity insomniacs – people who can't sleep! The night has very long, lonely, slow-moving hours for them.

At last I decided to see my GP. I didn't tell him about the pains in my stomach. No, just that I wasn't sleeping very well! He gave me some very light relaxing pills which at first did the trick. I was sleeping better, and the pains went for a few days, but then they were back again. What on earth was the matter? I began to fear the worst. Could it be that I had the disease we are all afraid to mention? Was I suffering from cancer? It was a shock even to say the word.

For a few more days I did absolutely nothing about it. I was too scared. I felt it was better to live in ignorance than to be told the truth, because by then I had convinced myself I had cancer. One evening I was invited to a party at which a friend of mind who was a first-class doctor was present. Dare I tell him? I gulped and took the plunge. I told him about the awful pains in my insides and that, even though I was ashamed to say it as a priest, I was scared of what it might be. He listened very sympathetically, giving me the odd nod of the head as I blurted out the details. He arranged to see me in his surgery two days later.

That period of waiting was the worst. At least while I was unsure I could pretend it wasn't cancer.

But once he had examined me professionally I would be told the truth. Could I take it? I had never been really ill in my adult life, except for a silly appendix removed twenty years before. The day dawned – the day of reckoning – and I drove with very mixed feelings to the surgery. He greeted me as a friend, but my heart was down in my boots. I hadn't the heart to respond to his friendship. One thing was certain, I would tell him the truth. And I did – the pains, the fear, the lack of sleep, the loss of appetite, my inordinate fear of cancer. He listened quietly.

For an hour he gave me the most thorough medical examination of my life. He pummelled my back, took my blood pressure, dug into my tummy with his fingers. I was x-rayed and then came the final result. I looked him in the eye. This was the moment of truth.

'My dear Michael,' he said, 'your tests all indicate . . .' He paused – what next? '. . . that you are a very healthy man.' I wanted to shout for joy. 'Your blood pressure is normal,' he continued, 'so are your kidneys. But I must warn you to take things a little easier. You are not as young as you used to be and you are doing far too much. This is causing you tension, and because you have a sensitive tummy this is where the tension shows itself.'

I pumped his hand in gratitude and shot out of the door like an olympic sprinter. The sky was blue, the sun was shining, and everything looked fresher and brighter. At least, I thought so. Of course, things had not really changed on the outside; what had changed was inside me. I left my fear behind me in the doctor's surgery. Oh, the pains in my stomach have gone, thank God, so have the pills. I am trying to slow down, but I'm afraid I'm not making a very good job of it.

For me the truth had to be faced, and when it was, my fear disappeared. There is an old saying which is a favourite of mine – I don't know who wrote it.

> Fear knocked at the door.
> Faith answered.
> There was no one there.

So, when we are afraid we have to learn to face the fear head-on and bring it out in the open. Then it will lose its hold over us. Jesus was afraid in the Garden of Gethsemane; he did not want to suffer the agony of the cross. So he prayed to his Father, and he was given the courage to face the cruelty of the Roman soldiers and the insults of the Jewish leaders. He was at peace within himself once he had conquered his fear. So I suggest that today you might look at something in your life which is causing you fear. Pray about it. Ask Jesus to help you, and he, who knew fear and conquered it within himself, will help you to do the same.

God, my Father, I turn to you in my unrest because I cannot see any way out of the present conflict which troubles my spirit. In my confusion I turn to you for help and guidance, because you alone can help me, and nothing is impossible to you. Light up my life with faith, and give me the courage to walk confidently where you would lead me. You know the right time to lift the burden that oppresses me, and so I place the present moment, as I do my whole life, in your tender care. Put your rest in my mind, and your peace in my heart.

Loving Yourself

Walk while you have the light, or the dark will overtake you. While you still have the light, believe in the light, and you will become sons of light. (John 12: 35–6)

The most important person to love is yourself. But, because we are damaged people, we have also to forgive ourselves. This means that we have to love ourselves as we are, warts and all. Strange as it may seem we often find it easier to blame rather than forgive ourselves. That is what prevents the real self from coming to the surface.

Take Peter for instance. 'All my life,' he told me, 'I have felt that I was living an unreal life. I never got to know the real "Me" because those around me never encouraged me to be myself. My father wanted me to be a "chip off the old block", and there was a pattern of behaviour in my home to which I had to conform for the sake of peace. I did well in business where "image" is important. I married and had a fairly happy family life until I noticed that I too was manipulating my children at an early age to conform to an image I wanted them to project. Now I realize that if I am to make any-

thing of my life I must get to know the real me.'
Peter is typical of hundreds whom we meet and try
to help in our healing services. Gradually, through
prayer and positive heart-searching, he began to
realize that God loved, and loves, him as a person
as he is. God does not select bits of us to love. He
reads our hearts. We may not love ourselves
because our vision is limited to 'mirror, mirror on
the wall'. We only see the outward appearances.
God is much more merciful on us than we are on
ourselves.

The thing that Peter found hardest to accept was
that God the Father had never stopped loving him
and never would. This awareness, as it became
clearer to Peter, was the source of his healing. It
helped him to look at himself, his wife and family,
his friends and God in a new way. It opened up a
whole new world for him. He trusted himself and
his life to God his loving Father. He gradually shed
his guilt feelings and was patient enough to realise
that his healing would take place gradually. In the
process of letting God's light shine on his life there
were periods of pain and withdrawal. In those
periods Peter felt very wobbly because he knew
that the healing of 'people becoming themselves'
requires time and great sensitivity which are as
necessary as in the treatment of an alcoholic or a
drug addict.

In our search for ourselves we will discover parts
within us which we have damaged in previous
years. We have to learn to look kindly on these,
knowing that God is our merciful father who

forgives us because he loves us. The past is part of us and its painful memories must be healed and soothed by God's love.

Peter is today a changed person and lives a full, whole life. 'When I realized that God loved me,' he said, 'I had to return in memory and forgive my father. He is long since dead, but now I feel sorry for him and for how much he missed in life. If only we had the chance over again perhaps things would have been different, but the past is dead, and I leave it to God's mercy. I have hurt so many people by my selfishness, especially my wife and family, but now I make amends not by looking back, but by living each day to the full. And what a challenge that is.'

There is a Peter in all of us. However honest and healed we are, there is still more healing to be done deep inside us. We have to allow God's light to shine on the darkened areas of our lives and gradually, through his help, we will become the type of person, not only that we want, but that God wants as well. We will be real people who can say, 'I'm glad I'm me.'

Father, I thank you for knowing and loving me better than I know myself, and for allowing me to know myself better than others know me. Heal me, I pray, by making me better than they suppose, and forgive my faults which they do not know, so that by trusting in you I may become the person you would have me be.